OPTIONS TRADING

For Beginners

By reading this document, the reader agrees that under no circumstances is the author responsible for any losses, direct or indirect, that are incurred as a result of the use of information contained within this document, including, but not limited to, errors, omissions, or inaccuracies.

Table of Contents

Introduction

The story of the stock market is one of booms and busts. Almost every generation has seen a major market crash, with those born in the eighties having witnessed three major crashes and one near miss. While the major themes behind all of these crashes were the same, one of greed and a lack of proper risk management, the underlying issue with the markets has always been that you need to adopt a direction in order to profit.

What I mean by this is that you have to either be long or short with regards to your positions. While there's only one way of making money in the markets, buying low and selling high, the order in which you do them places you firmly in a particular direction and this is where your risk compounds.

Stop loss orders and such are guards against this risk but there's not much use for a stop loss level if the market simply jumps the level. This is becoming a more common phenomenon these days thanks to the advent of algorithmic trading where the market can potentially move thousands of points in a few seconds. This phenomenon is also called a flash crash.

If anything, as time goes by, the markets look like they are becoming even more unstable places despite the increasing complexity of financial instruments available. So what is a novice, retail trader like yourself to do? Should you simply not trade at all?

Absolutely not! Whatever the forces operating in the market may be, the fact remains that financial markets are still some of the fairest and open in terms of competition. You see, it doesn't matter how much money you have behind a position or an instrument, ultimately everyone is equal in the market. The amount of money you make is equal to your skill and expertise, that's it.

Thus, the higher your skill and the better you manage your risk, the more the market will reward you. Successful trading really is about those two elements: your technical skills and your ability to manage risk. While technical skill is a function of how well you can read the market, the risk is a whole different ball game.

There are no in-depth manuals on how to manage your position risk. A lot of traders think of this as placing a stop loss order equivalent to a loss of a low percentage of their account and leave it at that. This is not even the tip of the iceberg when it comes to this topic.

The best way to manage risk is to simply be neutral in the market. In other words, to not be committed to either direction. How is this possible, you ask? Well, this is where options come in.

Options are a wonderful derivative which you can use to simply automate your risk management and thus get back to the task of focusing on what the market is actually doing. Now, you may have heard of how derivatives are the devil's work and so on but options are far from the financial WMDs that roam the marketplace these days.

At their heart, options are all about risk management and in some cases, completely eliminating the risk altogether. The strategies I will show you in this book work and have worked for a long time simply because they're evergreen and they utilize the power of options extremely well.

Some of them have complicated names, like straddles and strangles, but don't worry, their names are the only complicated part of all this. As you read this book, you will gain a new appreciation of the art of trading options and you will learn how, in some cases, you can even leave your portfolio to rest and not even check what the market is doing.

The inevitable question then arises: How much money can you make? Well, successful options traders usually rake in close to 50% per year on their capital, with the numbers being higher in institutions where leverage is employed. However, you should not be focusing on this number as a target.

Indeed, at this stage, this would be detrimental to your progress. Simply look at that number as what is possible and then get down to work understanding what options are. If you can nail the basics, you'll be well on your way to success since these strategies require a good understanding of the basics.

So without further ado, let's begin! We'll start off at the very beginning: What is an option?

Chapter 1: The Basics

An option is a type of derivative instrument that is freely traded in the market. A derivative instrument is one which derives its value from an underlying instrument. In the case of an option, this underlying instrument is the stock. Thus, the value of the option depends on the behavior of the stock.

Options do have an element of leverage in them, in that every lot of an option contains one hundred underlying shares of the common stock. For some instruments, this might be different but generally, this is the case. Simply trading options doesn't mean you limit your risk as explained in the introduction.

It is possible to have the possibility of an unlimited loss. The key lies in employing them the right way, just as any tool. There are two types of options which will be available to you as a retail trader, Calls and Puts.

Call and Put Basics

The technical definition of an option is that it gives the buyer the option to either buy or sell the underlying security but not the obligation****. In other words, if you own the option you can choose to either exercise it or not. The person selling you the option has no choice, they have to honor your request no matter what. It is for this reason that selling options is considered riskier than buying them.

A call gives you the right to buy the stock at a certain price and a put gives you the right to sell the stock at a certain price. A key thing to note here is that the option contract has its own price, which depends on a number of factors I'll shortly explain, and purchasing the contract doesn't mean you are purchasing the underlying stock.

It merely means that should you choose to exercise the option; you will be exercising it in lots of one hundred shares. For example: if you buy a call option for $X and later choose to exercise it, you still need to pay whatever the cost of the one hundred shares are.

An option contract has certain elements to it which determine its price. Let's take a look at these.

Contract Elements

An option contract has three elements to it: the strike price, the option type, and the expiry date. The strike price is not to be confused with the option contract price. The strike is simply the level beyond which the option comes 'into the money'. This is best explained via an example.

If you buy a call option for a stock, say AAPL, with a strike price of $160, this means you can buy the underlying stock at any time prior to its expiry. Since you've bought a call option, ideally you want the stock's market price to be greater than the strike price. This way, you can buy the stock at the lower option strike price and sell it at the higher market price. Thus, the call option is in the money in such a scenario.

For a put, on the other hand, you can only make money when the underlying market price is lower than the option's strike price. So, if you purchased an AAPL put with a strike price of $160, you can only make money when the stock is trading for less than $160. It is only in this scenario that the put is in the money. Hence, the strike price is the price which the market price must cross, the direction depends on whether the option is a call or a put, in order for you to make money on the option.

Next up is the expiry date. Options contracts don't exist forever, they expire at certain periods. The most common expiry date for an option is the last trading day of a month. Options usually exist for month long periods although there are some cases where they may exist for longer periods, sometimes years. These longer options are call LEAPS and are not the subject of our discussion in this book.

When you pull up quotes for an options contract in your broker's terminal, you will usually see contracts for three expiry dates: the current month, the next month (near month) and the month after that (the far month). Trading volumes are the greatest for current and near month options, with near month volumes gradually increasing as the current month's expiry date draws closer.

As the name, expiry date, suggests, the contract is not valid beyond this date and must be exercised either on or before this date. This brings us to the type of option. There are two types available: American and European. American options are more widely available and are preferred as trading instruments due to the fact that they can be exercised on any day prior to the expiry date.

By contrast, European options can be exercised only on the expiry date and not prior, and obviously not after. As you can imagine, this isn't very ideal for a trader since your chances of being right are greater over a period of time, like with the American option, as opposed to a day.

The next thing you ought to familiarize yourself with is the option contract ticker. The ticker for a contract is an amalgam of information so let's break this down. I'm going to use an actual example here.

AAPL190607C00150000 is an option that is currently trading at $25.60 with strike price of 150 and expiring on June 7th. This is a call option. Here's how this is broken down:

AAPL- this is the underlying stock's symbol, in this case, Apple Inc.

190607- this is the expiry date listed in yy/mm/dd format. Hence, June 7th, 2019.

C- This indicates this is a call option. A put would be denoted by a P.

00150000- This is the strike price represented as five digits prior to the decimal and three after. In this case, it is 00150.000 or $150.

Similarly, AAPL190607P00145000 is a put option on AAPL, expiring on 7th June 2019, with a strike price of $145.

Terminology

Options do have a language of their own and you will need to learn what these terms mean if you are to be successful. Below are the most commonly used terms for calls and puts.

- At the money- If the underlying stock's market price equals the option strike price, the option is at the money.

- Out of the money- The market price is beyond the strike price, greater than the strike price for a call and lesser than strike price for a put.

- Open interest- This number is the total volume of outstanding contracts. The higher this number is the greater the sentiment is for a particular price level.

- Intrinsic value- An in the money option has inherent value over an out of the money option. This value is the difference between the strike price and the stock's market price. (Market price-strike price in case of a call).

- Time value- Let's say a call option with a strike price of $10 is selling for $5, assuming the market price is 12$. In this case, the intrinsic value is $2. The remaining $3 is said to be the time value, or the premium you pay for the distance remaining till the expiry date. The further away the expiry date is, the greater the time value.

- Implied Volatility- Also called implied vol, this is a measure of the underlying volatility of the stock. This number is taken into consideration when calculating the option price. The greater the implied vol, the greater the price increase in the option.

- Delta- The rate of change of an option contract's price as the underlying stock price changes. For example, if the underlying increases in price by $1 and the call option increases in price by 2$, the delta is 2.

Instruments and Position Types

Options that are derived from stocks are the most commonly traded contracts. However, there are options available on FX pairs as well. Usually, these options are only available to institutional traders but a few international brokers do offer them. Some brokers even offer a CFD, which is a type of derivative that mimics another's movement, on options.

As a US resident, it is unlikely you will be accepted as a customer by an international broker and no US broker offers options on FX. Hence, it's best for you to stick to equity options, despite the vagaries of the stock market. By vagaries, I mean greater HFT presence which leads to flash crashes and the like. The FX market is far more volatile but due to the way the market is structured, traditional HFT strategies do not work in them and hence, price doesn't jump around as much.

This is not to say that FX is easier or safer in any way. In fact, thanks to leverage, the possibility of loss is greater. However, a lot of experienced traders prefer the FX market for the reasons outlined above.

So what sort of positions can you establish with options? A position is simply your trade in the market. As long as your trade is running, you have an open position and once you close the trade, you have closed your position. Briefly, there are four types of positions you can establish with options:

- Long call- This is when you buy a call option. You would do this if you believe the instrument's price is due for a rise beyond the option's strike price. Once it rises, you can exercise the option and sell the stock for a profit, sell the call option itself or let the option expire. If you let it expire, you lose your initial investment, which is the price you paid for the option. Obviously, if the option is in the money, you shouldn't be doing this.

- Long put- This is when you buy a put. If you believe the market price of the instrument is due to fall below the strike price, then having the right to sell the stock is invaluable. This way, once you exercise your put, you would sell the stock at the strike price and buy it back at the lower market price, sell the option itself or let the put expire. Again, if it is in the money, you don't want to do this.

- Short call- A short position on an option is established when you sell an option. Option sellers are also referred to as option writers since you're effectively writing the contract. In this case, you believe the stock will not rise beyond the strike price and are looking to pocket the option contract price or premium, that the call buyer will pay you. If it does move past the strike price, you must sell the stock to the option buyer if they exercise the option.

- Short put- Selling a put option establishes a short put position. In this case, you believe the market will not go below the option strike price. If it does go below, you are obligated to buy the stock from the option buyer at the option strike price. Remember, the put buyer sells the stock so you, as the put seller, buy it from them.

Short positions on options are fraught with risks and your broker will not allow you to establish such positions unless it is part of a larger strategy. In other words, standalone short option positions are unlikely to be approved. This is because of the risk they pose in case things go against you.

You will need higher levels of capitalization as well as trading experience for the broker to approve you trading such positions. An exception is made for covered short positions. This refers to you having the underlying stock in your possession prior to initiating the short. Thus a short call situation where you don't have ownership of the underlying stock is referred to as a 'naked' position.

Naked short calls and puts will almost never be approved by your broker unless you have a long relationship with them or bring a substantial amount of capital to the table. As a beginner, it is best to view standalone option shorts for informational purposes and not worry about actually trading these. So which scenarios are option shorts permissible in?

In the market, you can have two types of trading strategies. The first is directional strategies, which are the most commonly available. The second is spread strategies which are direction neutral. These strategies are extremely complicated to pull off with stocks but options make them a piece of cake.

So let's look at these in detail.

Spread Trading

As mentioned in the introduction, establishing a long or a short in the market requires you to commit to a definite direction in the market. You expose yourself to its vagaries and the risks that that entails. Now, directional trading will bring you the greatest amount of profit, no doubt. However, the price you pay for this greater profit is increased risk.

Spread trading, on the other hand, gives you lower profits per trade and takes a little longer to play out. However, the lack of risk makes it an extremely attractive option for keeping your gains over the long term. All spread trading strategies involve buying an option and selling a related option which is different either in strike price or its expiry date.

Spread trading strategies' returns depend on the sort of risk you're willing to take. It's not a good idea to throw the value of returns around since so much depends on the individual trader but an elite options trader can expect to make somewhere between 50-100% on their capital.

Again, as a beginner, you should not aim for such numbers but simply use it for inspiration and focus instead on learning the basics as outlined in this book. Spread trading strategies also allow you to do something which you cannot on directional trades: adjust your position. This is what makes them so powerful against adverse market conditions and this is how you protect your downside on the fly.

Either way, spread trading is possibly the best philosophy with which to approach the markets. A lot of beginners tend to go directional, thanks to the higher profit potential or out of simple ignorance. However, you will find a lot of professional traders adopt as neutral a position on the market as possible since this is more reliable a method in the long run.

Now that we've covered the basics, you might be thinking it's time to move on to the good stuff and sink your teeth into the strategies! Wrong. You still need to learn a few more basics with regards to money management. Money and risk management are crucial for your success and this is detailed in the next chapter.

Chapter 2: Risk Management

Money and risk management doesn't get nearly enough attention as it ought to, in my opinion. This is because it's far sexier to talk about fancy strategies and show people how much money they can make. However, risk management is what underlines everything in trading and is what will make sure you keep your money in the long run.

Understand this: It's very easy to make money in the markets. That's right. There's no shortage of traders who make 100% gains per month. Keeping this money is a completely different matter though. Those 100% gains traders usually wipeout after a month or two thanks to improper risk and money management.

In this chapter, I will show you basic money management techniques. By adopting these, as unglamorous as they might seem, you will put yourself ahead of virtually 90% of the traders out there. That's traders. Not just beginners.

Risk

What exactly is risk? Well, to define it at its most basic level, it is simply the probability of you losing your money on a particular trade. Now, the key word here is probability. There are a number of things that affect the probability of your trade being a win or a loss. So let's look at these and see how you can reduce the risk associated with these individual items.

Technical Strategy

Your technical strategy refers to your entry and exit system in the market. When will you enter and at what level will you exit? Is your entry signal based on sound market principles? This second point is more of a concern for directional strategies since a lot of them tend to be discretionary. With spread trading strategies, as you will see, a lot of this guesswork is taken out of the equation and thus, your risk is automatically lowered.

Exits are something that a lot of traders don't spend a lot of time thinking about. You need to define exactly which levels you will exit the trade at and under what conditions. Then there's the small matter of exiting consistently at profitable levels. In fact, it's best to deal with exits as a separate section entirely.

Exits

There are three kinds of exits you can take in the market. A win, a loss, or a scratch/break even. The first two types of exits should be your major focus since the third will take care of itself through your trading plan, which I'll talk about in a later chapter.

With directional strategies, your downside is limited by a stop loss order, which is just a way of saying 'if the market goes below this level, close out my position.' With spread trading, there is no stop loss order involved. Instead, we need to focus on the maximum loss amount of a trade.

This maximum loss amount should be a function of our overall account size, expressed as a percentage. Generally speaking, as a beginner trading option spreads, you should not risk more than 1% of your overall account size per trade. This means, if you have an account size of $10,000, you should not lose more than $100 per trade.

Furthermore, you need to keep this risk percentage consistent across every single trade. If you take a loss on your first trade and lose $100, then your overall account size is now $9900 and thus, your new maximum risk per trade is $99. Keep this percentage consistent at all times.

Your average profit percentage should be tied to your per trade risk percentage, usually a multiple of this. So if you risk 1% per trade, aim to make at least 2%

per win, or double your risk every time you win. Now, it is not necessary for you to stick to a 2X multiple as a win target. The exact multiple is determined by your win percentage.

Your win percentage is the number of trades you make money on divided by the total number of trades. It is here that most beginners trip themselves up by chasing the highest win percentage. This is understandable since we've been conditioned since our school days to chase the highest percentage of correct answers in any task.

The thing is, the market does not work that way. You can win nine out of ten trades or 999 out of 1000 and still lose money. Think about it: if you lose an amount greater than your wins on that single trade, all of your previous 'correct' answers are for naught. This is why it is essential for you to keep your risk percent consistent on every single trade you take.

Your money-making ability is governed by two things, mathematically speaking. Your win percentage and your average win amount. You can have a low win percent but if your average win amount is high enough to eliminate all your losses, then you're making money and it doesn't matter that you didn't get enough answers 'correct'.

Similarly, if you have a higher win percentage then you can afford to have a lower average win amount. The process of determining which average win levels you need to target for a corresponding win percent is something that happens over time. What most traders do is start off by targeting a 2X multiple on risk for an average win and after on hundred trades, evaluate to see if they could have pocketed bigger gains and how that would have affected the win percentage.

The key, as ever, is consistency. While it might be easy to take an immediate profit and vow to take a larger one the next time in order for your average win to remain the same, this is the wrong way to approach things. Ensure your median and mean are the same, statistically speaking. Statistics play an important role in risk management, as we shall see next.

Drawdowns

While your risk per trade and your exits can be controlled by you, your equity curve's direction depends, largely, on the markets. This is because it is possible to do everything right in trading and still lose money. After all, this is why traders need to consider the odds of their strategy and not the certainty with which things might happen.

Your equity curve is the best measure of how well your strategy is playing out, no matter how good or bad it looks on paper. The drawdown is perhaps the most relevant portion of the equity curve. A drawdown refers to a dip in the equity curve. The maximum drawdown is the biggest dip your equity curve experiences.

You ought to measure the max drawdown both in size (amount), percent of your account equity, as well as time. This last one is important since you will be comparing this time to the time it takes your account to erase this drawdown and make new equity highs again.

This second time period is called the recovery period and if it is longer than the drawdown period, your strategy isn't very practical, no matter how much money it makes. This is because over the long run, you won't end up making much money or will have to wait longer periods to recover your capital, thanks to the slow recovery process your strategy undertakes.

Durability is another aspect you need to consider. While there isn't a fixed number or even measurement to pinpoint durability, you can think of it as a measure of how many trades your system needs to make money on in order to be successful. For example, a 20% win rate system with an average win of 5X risk is more durable than a 70% win rate system with an average win of 1X risk.

This is because the first system only needs to be correct 20% of the time to make money, whereas the second needs to be right 70% of the time. Also, you can bet that the recovery period of the first system is going to be many multiples faster than the drawdown period.

A lot of professional traders will opt for the first system, while beginners will flock to the second. This, by itself, should make it obvious as to which type of system you should be after. This is not to say that you should design a low win rate and high average win system on purpose. Merely, that chasing after high win rates is missing the point of what trading is about completely.

Your only purpose is to find a combination of a profitable win rate and average win, make sure it has a recovery period that is faster than a drawdown period and then execute that strategy as many times as possible. The more you execute it, the more money you will make since the odds will play out better.

Other Measurements

The numbers discussed above are the basic risk numbers you should be tracking at all costs. Beyond this, there are a number of other statistics such as the maximum adverse excursion, maximum favorable excursion, the sharpe ratio, and so on.

These are not particularly important since they're just a reflection of what you're doing in the markets. All of them are a function of the basic measurements I listed above so make sure you are as consistent as possible in your execution and the rest will take care of itself.

Just to make it clear, risking the correct account percent per trade is a part of successful execution. Taking proper exits is a part of execution. Don't make the mistake of thinking that simply following your entry signal is successful execution.

Other Forms of Risk

While there are elements of risk that can be measured, there are some forms of risk that are qualitative in nature. This refers to your routines and your preparation prior to sitting down to trade. How consistent you are with these routines will determine your success in the markets.

Prep Routine

How will you prepare for the market before sitting down to trade? Will you exercise physically? Mentally? Think of yourself as a professional athlete before sitting down to trade. Have you ever seen an athlete change his or her routine prior to a game? Unlikely. They always go through the same warm-up sequence in a highly structured and organized manner.

You need to do the same before you trade. You cannot expect to roll up after a session at the local bar with your buddies and expect to trade successfully. Neither can you trade hungover or when you're depressed or dealing with some major life situations.

Scheduling some time off from the markets is essential to remaining fresh. A lot of traders get greedy and think they need to remain in the market at all times. This is simply not true. You can execute your strategy only if you're fully fresh and time away from the screen is essential for this. This doubly applies if you have a full-time job, as most readers of this book likely have.

A good idea before sitting to trade is to meditate. Getting physical exercise is also a great way to make sure your mind is fresh. Make sure you've eaten well and keep any other distractions to a minimum. This includes any CNBC or financial channel which is full of useless information anyway.

Remind yourself of why it is you wish to trade and what benefits you expect it to bring if done successfully. Feel this emotion as you sit down and then begin your analysis of the markets.

Trade at the same time whenever you do decide to trade. This is because the market will have a different dynamic depending on the time of day and the more you're exposed to a particular type of volatility and liquidity, the better it will be for you. So don't chop and change and sit down whenever you feel like it. This will build inconsistency within you and is bad for your long-term performance.

Session Routines

So you've analyzed the market and have spotted a couple of opportunities which haven't come to fruition as of yet. You'll need to wait for a while before this happens. What will you do in the meantime? Will you browse the internet? Will you finish your errands around your home? Will you stare at the screen like a zombie?

Your task is to stay focused but not obsessively so since this will build fatigue. A good idea is to read a book or something else that keeps your mind engaged but not distracted to the point where you forget about the market and potentially miss your entry point.

Once you enter a trade, what are you going to do? Will you watch over it obsessively, even it if needs no management? Will you count every tick for and against you? Needless to say, this sort of attachment will burn you out within a few days and if you do suffer from this, it points to a lack of understanding of the market's nature.

By thinking that every single trade's result matters, you're ignoring the fact that the odds play out over a series of trades and not just a few. Therefore, you don't really need to care about results as long as you execute properly and consistently. Indeed, consistency is what makes money, not fancy strategies.

If you don't find any entry opportunities, what are you going to do? Will you switch off your terminal and do something else? Will you practice your skills? Will you refine your strategy in some manner? Define all of these things before you ever place a single trade. I'll talk about all of this in the chapter on building your trading plan, but for now, start thinking about the point I'm trying to make here.

The point is about focus. Trading calls for a lot of it, even when there's no action around. A lot of trading time is spent sitting around waiting for a good entry. It is only then that there's some activity followed by another long session of doing nothing but monitoring and adjusting. Activity when it does occur, happens in short bursts and you need to accept the fact that, for the most part, you'll be sitting around doing nothing.

Thus, if excitement is what you're looking for, skydiving might be a better career choice.

Post Session Routines

What will you do after the session is finished? Will you review your actions? Or will you take a break and do it later? Do you think you will be able to review your trades if you've experienced a tough session?

It's not possible to answer all of these up front but have a plan going in and then be honest with yourself about what you need to do. Generally, I advise reviewing daily as well as weekly. In the beginning, your rate of learning is going to be very high so you'll literally be a different trader by the end of the week, thanks to the knowledge you'll be absorbing.

The post trade or post session environment is when

it's a good idea to reinforce the fact that it is not the individual trade but the consistency of your execution over thousands of trades that will make you money. It is possible to do everything right and still lose money. Indeed, making money on a single trade is simply a matter of luck.

However, over a large number of trades, the odds come into play and making money over them is skill. So focus on the longer term and bigger picture. The money will take care of itself.

Hopefully, you can see by now how important consistency is and why this is so. While there are a lot of risk factors you can control over the long run, in the short term you are exposed to the vagaries of the market. There is some risk here as well that you can mitigate; however, by changing the type of orders you place in the market.

This depends on your choice of broker so let's take a look at this next, along with the regulations and rules you'll need to abide by if you wish to trade options.

Chapter 3: Your Broker

Question: Who is the only person in the market that always makes money? It's your broker! The middleman who takes a small cut of every trade you make does have to fulfill a number of capital and regulatory requirements but the adage that the best business in the stock market is to be a broker is very true.

This doesn't mean to say that you ought to consider your broker your enemy. Far from it. It's just that you must understand your broker's primary duty is to execute your order. It is not to recommend or advise you on how to trade or what to buy or sell. So don't be picking up the phone asking for advice from such an entity, no matter what the marketing says.

Brokers will require you to satisfy a number of requirements prior to being able to trade. Let's look at these now.

Types

Brokers can be roughly divided into two types, and no I don't mean as weasels and even bigger weasels. I'm referring to full service and discount brokers. A full-service broker usually has financial advisors on board who can help you out with your retirement account and such. These brokers usually have phone service which you can call to place your trades and such.

A discount broker adopts a more bare-bones approach. Aside from a trading terminal, you're unlikely to receive anything else. While discount brokers these days have sophisticated trading interfaces, a full-service broker will always be a better bet if your account size is large.

By large, I mean anything north of half a million dollars in capital. Below this amount, a discount broker is your best bet.

Margins

The amount of capital in your account is referred to as your margin. Within the US, there are two kinds of trading accounts, referred to as cash and margin. Note that the account type named 'margin' does not refer to your capital but simply to your ability to borrow money from your broker.

With a cash account, the only thing you can do is go long on stocks. In order to go short, you will need to borrow stock from your broker and this requires you to have a margin account to do so. Some brokers impose higher account minimums for margin accounts. Even if you do manage to get past this hurdle, there's still the government you need to deal with.

The bane of many a beginner trader is the PDT or pattern day trader rule. This rule classifies anyone who executes four or more trades within a five-day period, as a pattern day trader. Anyone who is classified as such needs to maintain a minimum balance of at least $25,000.

A lot of beginner traders get cute with this rule and try to stick to just a cash account, that is placing long stock trades, in order to trade with lower capital amount. This is simply shooting yourself in the foot since it is unlikely you'll ever make much money this way. You need to go long as well as short to be successful and you can never know when you need to exit.

Over and above this, you need a margin account to even trade options. Thus, it is best if you begin trading with at least $25,000 in capital. If you don't have this much capital, then make plans to raise it. It really isn't worth trying to trade in the US with less than this amount since you'll have to compromise somehow or the other and this leads to inefficient trading which will lose you money.

Margin Call

A margin call occurs when you do not have enough equity in your account to cover your margin requirements. Your account's equity is the sum of its cash balance and the value of any outstanding positions. Brokers require you to have what is called maintenance margin as long as your position is open.

With stock trades, the margin requirements are pretty straightforward, with 25% usually being deemed appropriate. When it comes to options spreads trading though, that calculation is a bit different. Usually, the margin you'll need to maintain when selling a put equals half the market value of the stock plus any credits received less the amount by which the option is out of the money.

Brokers will not let you sell naked calls or put at the beginning. In fact, it is unlikely that some will even let you sell calls even when you have the underlying stock in your possession unless you have a high account balance. This requirement varies by broker so check all of their terms and conditions before you sign up.

The other thing you must get used to is reading the price spread. You see, while CNBC and their ilk display a single price for a stock ticker, in reality, the price is actually comprised of two numbers, the bid and the ask. The bid, which is a lower number, represents the price at which you can sell the stock and the ask is the price at which you can buy it.

In order for your trade to make money then, the last traded price must cross the spread. This is why it is difficult to buy a stock and then sell it an instant later. The difference between the bid and the ask is called the spread. Technically, within the trading world, the difference between the two numbers is referred to as a spread, so this term is not confined to just price. However, it is most widely used in this regard.

Other Considerations

Most beginners assume they'll be able to get the price they see on screen automatically. However, there's this little thing called slippage which happens quite a lot in the market and you'll find forums full of beginner traders complaining about this as if a crime has been committed. The market is fast paced and more often than not, the price on your screen isn't always 100% accurate to the second.

In fact, the lowest unit of time the market can be measured in these days is a nanosecond, with HFT firms deploying hundreds of trades per millisecond. So, to expect the price to be exactly what you see on screen is unrealistic. This doesn't mean it's inaccurate, just that the market is too fast for you to accurately capture price to the exact value.

This is why you need to give your trades some room to breathe since if your profit targets are too close to your entry point, a single point's slippage will cost you many percentage points on your average win number and throw your math off kilter.

While slippage is a huge issue in directional trading, spread trading takes some of these risks out of the picture. Having said that, there is the issue of entering at a price that isn't very efficient. You can mitigate this by choosing to place certain types of orders though.

So let's look at the types of orders you can most likely place as a retail trader in the market.

Order Types

The days are long gone when you simply told your broker to buy this or sell that and they carried it out. A lot of brokers these days have a veritable arsenal of order types which can both help and hurt you. How you choose to deploy these will determine your success.

First off, we have the market order. The market order is an instruction to your broker to purchase or sell a security at whatever the market price is. It is with this type of order that slippage occurs the most since the market price changes quite a lot. If you're desperate to enter a position or if your profit target is far enough away that a few points slippage will not make much of a difference, then market orders are a good way to ensure your position size gets filled.

From a consistency perspective, this is important since a lower position size will throw your math and probabilities off and you'll have to extend your profit target to bring it back in line. However, slippage can be a real concern in times of extreme volatility. For such situations, we have the limit order.

A limit order places an instruction with your broker to buy or sell the security at a maximum price. Thus if you're going long, placing a limit order for 100 units at $40 will tell your broker to buy as many units of the instrument as possible, up to 100 units, at a price of $40 or lower. If you're shorting 100 units at $40 on a limit order, then your broker will look to sell the stock at $40 or higher.

The limit instruction essentially tells your broker to get the best price possible for a fixed number of units. The key point to remember is that if the price moves past the limit, into unfavorable territory, your full position will not be filled. Thus, if your broker could only find 50 units at $40 or better and if price jumped past $40, then your position size will remain at 50. You will now need to figure out how much extra you'll need to make in order to maintain your profitability calculations.

Since the lack of a guaranteed fill is a problem, brokers offer what is called a stop order. A stop order prioritizes filling the position above all else. It differs from a regular market order in that traders can place a trigger level on it. So, from the previous example, if you place a stop order to buy 100 units at $40, the

$40 price is a trigger. Once the market price, the ask, in this case, reaches this level, your broker will sell 100 units no matter what the price is. Contrast this to the limit where your broker will only sell if the price is above $40 and you can see the difference.

Do not confuse a stop order with a stop loss order. The stop loss is simply a name given for what the order achieves. You can have a stop loss order which is a limit order or a stop order. The stop loss is not an order 'type', it is the name given for an 'objective'.

Next up, we have the stop limit order which combines the limit and stop order types. In this case, once the trigger or limit is breached, the position will be activated as a stop order but until it is, the order behaves as a limit order. Generally speaking, you won't need to use this type of order too much.

Orders can also be defined in terms of how long they last. There are two types in this category: the GTC and the day order. GTC stands for good till canceled and this means the order stands valid until you cancel it yourself. A lot of traders sometimes forget about orders placed a while back and forget to cancel them. Don't be one of these traders.

A day order refers to one which will expire at the end of the market session. In the stock market, this refers to the end of the trading day but in the FX market, it means the order will expire at the end of the twenty-four hour worldwide session.

Another type of order is the fill or kill. This order lays

stress on filling the entire position at the specified price. If the entire quantity cannot be filled at the price given, then the broker need not purchase even a single unit of the instrument. In case the order cannot be filled, then it is automatically canceled.

A variation of this order is the all or none. With this, the execution priority is the same as the fill or kill but the order remains valid even if the broker cannot fill the order, unlike the fill or kill where it gets canceled.

There are a number of other orders, almost one hundred and thirty more, that are offered by brokers. Going by names such as icebergs and OTO and so on, the types of orders are almost endless and will make your head spin. You don't need to concern yourself with these order types since they're mostly used by professional traders and market makers.

Your focus should merely be on the orders mentioned previously and how you can use them to manage your risk.

Order Risk Management

While a lot of traders jump in and start placing market orders when they begin trading, the correct approach is one which embraces all three order types; market, limit and stop. Each order has its own vagaries and you should deploy the one which suits the environment the best.

Your first step should be to determine your reward point or amount. If it is large enough and if the market's current volatility is not going to affect your profitability calculations too much, then the market order is your best bet. Situations where the market is not going to be volatile or where you might not be present at the screen, demand a limit order.

Some clarification is needed here. When entering a position, always use a limit order if you happen to be away from the screen. This is especially a concern for those trading FX since there's no earthly reason you should be in front of a screen for an entire day. If you do happen to employ stop loss orders, which you will not need if you follow the strategies in this book, they should always be stop orders since your objective should be to get out of the position at all costs.

When in front of the screen you can use either market or limit orders as per your judgment. Despite seeming complex, after some screen time, you'll be able to judge this for yourself so don't worry about nailing it the first few times.

This concludes our look at brokers and the types of orders you can use. Thus far, we've gone about establishing a base from which you can trade successfully. Remember that risk management is what comes first. Above all else, as a beginner, your mindset should first be geared towards survival and only then should you bother with trying to make money.

The most successful traders are those who have played the game the longest. While playing for a long time requires you to make money, the fact is that you can't make any money if you don't have any capital. So seek to preserve your capital at all costs by risking a very small percentage of your account per trade.

Build a good base and once you've gained experience, expand your strategies and number of instruments traded and you'll find yourself among the successful select few who make it in the markets.

So with having gotten all of that out of the way, let's start diving into options trading strategies.

Chapter 4: Covered Calls

We first begin by looking at an evergreen strategy which is perfect for those who already hold stock in some companies, either through a regular brokerage or retirement account. A lot of prospective traders enter the market after dabbling in it via retirement portfolio investing so it makes sense to leverage this into an options strategy.

Selling covered calls, as a strategy, has been around for ages now and it is important to note that this is not a trading strategy in and of itself. It is best to view it as an extension of your investment activity.

The Method

How would you like to decrease the cost you incurred when you paid for the stock you purchased? Let's say you purchased 200 shares of AAPL for $100 each. This total purchase cost you $20,000, which is quite a substantial sum. If you could reduce this value by even a little, then whatever profits you make from your AAPL investment will only be magnified.

This is where selling covered calls comes in.

What is it?

Selling a naked call is a bad idea, as we've seen previously. This is because your theoretical loss is unlimited. After all, if you're selling a call, you're betting on the price of a security decreasing. However, if it goes against you, then the price to which it could rise is unlimited, no matter how high your strike price.

This is why your broker will not allow you to sell naked calls unless you have the capital and the experience to do so. Covered calls; however, solve the issue of risk because with this strategy, you'll be writing calls for stock you already own.

The crux of the covered call income strategy is the time decay factor. When an option is priced, the time left to expiry is taken into account. When an option still has ninety days left to expire, it's premium (cost) will still be relatively high even if it's out of the money. However, an option that is closer to expiry and out of the money will have a very small premium since it simply has less time to move into the money.

The option that is further out has greater time to do so. As it moves closer to its expiry and remains out of the money, it's chances of moving in the money decline. With this comes the decline in price which accelerates during the final sixty days of the option's life.

Thus by writing calls that are at least sixty-one days

out from expiry, you can take advantage of the decay in price, which is caused by time. Hence, the term time decay. Here's how you execute this strategy,

Execution Steps

Remember this strategy assumes you have already found a stock that you would like to go long on. Ideally, this stock is an investment decision and you're looking to own this stock for a long time. Covered calls will generate income for you while you hold this stock.

Let's assume you've bought 200 AAPL at $100. Your cost per share is $100 and let's say the market price is currently $175 (which it is at this time of writing). This puts you in a nice profit of $75 per share. Not bad at all.

Once you have your long position established, on the stock, your next step is to hunt for an out of the money call which is at least sixty-one days away. Usually, I prefer an option that expires after the far month. This is because the far month options will already have some time decay effects built into them.

As of this writing, the $180 strike price AAPL call options expiring in the far month are trading at $7.83 and the ones expiring the month after are trading at $9.45. That's an additional $2 per share which is quite significant.

Once you've identified the suitable expiry date for options, you need to then decide on an appropriate strike price. This is often the tricky bit since you'll have to balance the option premium (which will be your income) versus the possibility that the stock may rise past that level. Your ideal scenario in this strategy is to keep holding onto the long stock position and have your options you wrote expire out of the money.

This is usually a judgment call and you should use technical analysis and some basic fundamental analysis to determine the appropriate strike price. I'll cover this in later chapters but for now, all I can say is there's no template for this. No one can predict how much a stock will rise. The best course for beginners to take is to write well out of the money options and hope for the best.

So, in this example, let us write options for a strike price of $205. This is $50 away from our current market price and represents a 28.5% price increase, which seems unlikely over a three-month period. Currently, the call is selling for $2.06. Given our long position of 200 shares, we will write two contracts, since each contract covers 100 shares.

Thus, if AAPL doesn't move past $205, we'll end up earning $410 over the next three months. Effectively, what we've done is, we've reduced our per share cost of AAPL by $2.06, which is the option premium we earn. Assuming we earn a premium throughout the lifespan of the long position, AAPL can actually dip below our original purchase price and we'll still be in a profit.

Considerations

What if AAPL does go past $205? Well, in that case, you will have to sell your position in AAPL. Given that you bought the stock at $100, this means you lock in a $105 per share profit which is a tidy sum, to say the least, despite the position going against you.

If AAPL dips below $100 then you'll profit from your option position and earn that premium. Your long position is in a loss now but since you had planned on holding onto the position for a while anyway, presumably you'd be okay with this. Meanwhile, you can continue writing calls.

The only scenario in which you would lose money with this strategy is if you sold your AAPL for below your purchase price and if your option premiums could not cover the loss.

All of this gives us some important lessons and things to watch out for when it comes to this strategy:

- Write calls only once your long position has moved into a reasonable profit. What is reasonable? Well, whatever makes sense to you. If your strike price is hit then you'll have to sell your stock position so presumably, this should be a number you're satisfied taking a profit at.

- Do not write calls if there is an expected announcement which could cause extreme volatility. Taking the AAPL example, avoid writing calls around the time of the Apple conferences when new products are revealed. If the company is under any special investigation, like Facebook often is, stay away. What you want is a nice old boring company like say, Coca Cola or Kimberly Clark.

- Choose a strike price that is far away and work your way inwards. You could even write one contract for a far away strike and one closer. You increase your risk but if your position is in a profit already, you have literally zero risk.

Other considerations should be the technical and fundamental nature of the stock in question which will be covered later so don't worry about this for now. As you can see, the covered call is an excellent strategy to utilize as a way to produce income on the stocks you already own. Not only will this reduce your initial purchase cost, or your cost basis, but also protect your downside should your long position go against you.

You could try this on speculative positions as well but given the ninety-day realization period, it's probably not a great fit.

Chapter 5: Collars

The collar is a step above, in terms of complexity, from a covered call. Indeed, you can think of this as being a combination of a protective put (where you purchase a put in lieu of a stop loss) and a covered call. Collars are extremely versatile, in that they require no day to day management and both the upside and downside are capped.

From a risk perspective then, collars are an ideal solution since no matter what the market does, you can rest assured your position is safe. However, the upside of a collar trade being capped does put a limit in your win amount if the position goes your way.

The Method

Collars involve three moving parts: a long stock position, a short call, and a long put. The strike price of the put is usually out of the money as is the strike price of the call. You want the put to be as close to the money as possible though, to cover your downside. As for the call, the same guidelines as in the covered call strategy apply.

You can use collars to generate a return either over

the short term or the long term, that is over a year. The long term will provide better returns, thanks to the lower tax rate your trading will attract.

What is it?

Collars are named thus because the put and the call cap both ends of your long trade and hence establish a collar of sorts around it. The idea behind this is that the put, which is a few points away out of the money from your long stock entry price, protects your downside.

However, your costs do increase thanks to the premium you will pay for the option. The closer the put is to the money, the greater its price will be. However, go too far out of the money and you increase your downside risk on the long position dramatically.

Meanwhile, selling the call gives you some income and this offsets some of the additional cost. Writing a call close to the money will give you a greater premium and maybe even finance the put purchase. However, the increased premium caps your upside that much more.

So, as you can see, it's a neutral strategy overall and you should not expect blockbuster gains with this. However, given the fixed risk and the lack of work it takes, collars should form the basis of your options trading strategy.

Execution Steps

As with the covered call, your first step is to establish a long position. Let's take the previous example of AAPL which is selling at $175.

Next, you should purchase your protective put. Let's fix our risk at five points and buy the far month 170 put which is selling for $7.70. Next, we write a far month 200 call for $1.83. Let's work the numbers now:

Our total cost to enter the trade= long stock cost+ put cost- call income= 175+7.7-1.83= 180.87. Thus to break even on this trade, the stock price has to move to at least $180.87.

What will our maximum loss be? Well, we have a protective put in place to cap our downside. Therefore, our max loss is the difference between the strike price of the put and our cost price:

Max loss= Cost of position- Put strike price= 180.87-170= 10.87

What is our maximum gain? Well, the call caps our gain so this number is going to be the strike price of the call subtracted from the cost price:

Max gain= Call strike price- Cost of position= 200-180.87=19.13

Thus, we stand to make $19.13 and lose $10.87 at the most. Given our investment of $180.87 plus commissions, this works out to a maximum gain of 10.5% and a maximum loss of 6%.

Given that this is a far month trade, the numbers are quite high. We're talking close to 11% gain on a single trade if things go our way. However, you'll notice that the downside is quite high as well. A loss of 6% over three months is a tad too high.

The way to reduce risk would be to buy a put as close to the current trading price as possible. Now the current price is $175.7 and not $175 which I assumed for calculation purposes.

The far month 175 put is currently selling at $9.60. Assuming the same call numbers as above, this reduces our cost basis to $182.77. Hence, our max loss is 4.2%. This is still a bit too high. However, we can't buy a put closer than 175.

Therefore, our only option is to write a call closer to the strike price. Given that we're talking about three months, a strike price of $190 seems reasonable. This represents an 8.5% rise which is within the volatility ballpark for AAPL. Note, I'm not saying it will go there, just that given how much the stock swings about, it seems reasonable to assume it will go there.

The $190 far month call is selling for $4. Thus, this gives us a new cost basis of $180.6. Our maximum loss is 3.1% which is quite manageable. Our maximum gain is 5.2% which is quite excellent for a three-month return on a single trade.

Considerations

The collar is a pretty stable strategy but it can be a bit difficult to nail down the exact amount of risk you wish to carry. Given the relatively lower levels of profits this strategy gives, it's better to apply this to longer term options of LEAPS. This way, you get to keep more of your gains thanks to the lower taxation.

The other consideration is, of course, which strike price you ought to choose for your calls and puts. Taking puts further away from your entry price increases your reward but also ramps up your risk. Given that your profit is capped, it's probably best to stick with a put that is as close as possible to your entry price, as in the example previously.

Another factor to consider is adjustment. If the price does fall far enough for the put to be in the money, should you hold the position or should you close the entire trade out? Opinion is divided as to what to do. On one hand, your long position should be established only because you're certain it is a worthwhile venture and so, a dip below your put shouldn't fluster you.

However, given that you won't necessarily be holding this position for the long term, that is, the long purchase is not an investment but is a speculation, it might be better to just take the loss and move on. The thing to do, therefore, is to make up your mind before you enter the trade. How long do you want to hold on to this trade? How long do you think you want to give the long stock position time to work out? This will also inform which call you wish to write.

Adjusting the trade is a simple trade since it's a simple matter of moving your collar downwards. Once price moves below your put, it will rise in value and your premium on the call is secured as well. Thus, you can close both the put and the call positions for a profit and this will offset the loss on the long stock position.

What you then do is initiate another collar, with a lower put strike price and write another call with a lower price. Thus, all you've done is move your collar downwards. If your original long thesis was correct, the price should bounce upwards soon enough and you will make an additional profit over and above your original projection.

Of course, there is the risk of the trade not working out, in which case you will have taken a bigger loss despite some of this loss being mitigated by the gains on the initial put. So fix your baseline firmly and if the price dips below this level then close out the trade and cap your risk.

This concludes our look at collars and as you can see, they're an excellent option and a steady money spinner. By being market neutral, you get to benefit from the lower risk exposure and are not exposed to the vagaries of a directional market.

Chapter 6: Call Spreads

Spread strategies are more advanced in that you don't need to establish a long position. Thus, the cost of establishing a position is a lot lower than with the covered call or the collar trade. While your long-term options trading base should be rooted in those strategies, pursuing spread trades will give you healthy returns in the short term.

Spread trades work very much in principle like collar trades except you will be buying and selling calls (or puts) of the same month and the same type of option in every trade. In other words, while you were selling calls and buying puts with the collar, in this case, you will be buying and selling calls or buying and selling puts.

This chapter will introduce you to call spreads.

Bull Call Spreads

One of the biggest benefits of trading options is that you don't need to be terribly worried about the current market situation since your trades are designed to profit in all markets. At the very least, you will have a strategy, no matter what the market is doing. The bull call spread, also called the long call spread, is a strategy for a moderate to strong bullish market.

In this scenario, you're quite certain that the stock is going to increase in value over the medium term but you're a bit uncertain about the volatility it is showing. You see, there is a dose of uncertainty with every directional position and you are compensated for this with higher rewards. Options strategies take this uncertainty away but cap your maximum reward.

Thus, if you're extremely certain that a stock is going to go upwards for sure, buying a long call is probably the best strategy. After all, if you know a stock is going to increase in value, why would you place a cap on your profits by writing a call at a higher strike price?

Such situations are extremely rare; however, and this is where the bull call spread comes into action.

How it Works

With the bull call spread, you will be buying a long call which is either in the money or close to the money and offsetting this price by writing an out of the money call. If the stock goes past the higher strike price, your long call is in profit but your overall profit is capped to the level of the higher strike price.

If the stock goes below your long call, you have the

premium of the higher strike price call to offset your loss, which is simply the premium you paid for the long call. Remember, you're not buying any stock in this strategy so there is no loss on the stock itself.

Let's continue to use AAPL as an example of this. As of this writing, AAPL is trading at $173.3. The closest at the money call option in the near month is the $170 and $175 which is trading at $6.95 and $4.10 respectively. Now, you could choose either of these strike prices. Remember, you're moderately bullish on the stock but are not sure how high it will go. Given these conditions, let's purchase the 175 call for $4.10.

Now, we need to find a suitable strike price to write a call at. This is a tricky balancing act. Write a call too far away and you won't receive enough of a premium. Write one too close, and you're not giving your trade enough breathing room. This is why it's essential to keep your time horizon on this trade as short as you can afford to. Ideally, your options will have some time value left on them but not too much time so as to bring price uncertainty into them.

The time decay is evident in the current month option prices. The $190 option is selling for $0.37 which is a pittance really. However, let's stick with the current month for now. So what do our risk and reward look like?

Maximum risk= Premium paid for long call- Premium received for short call= 4.1-0.37= 3.73.

Maximum reward= Strike price of short call- Strike

price of long call- cost paid for entering the trade= 190-175-3.73= 11.27

Thus our reward/risk on this 3X. Just to clarify, the prices quoted for an option contract are on a per share basis. Since every contract contains a hundred shares, you should multiply the price by a hundred to get the full price of the contract.

So, to enter this position, or to purchase a single contract, we will need to spend $373 and if the price hits our higher strike price of $190 then we'll clear $1127 on the trade. These numbers are with the near month options, of course. Let's look at how the numbers change by taking the far month into consideration.

Price of far month $175 call= $6.30

Price of far month $190 call= $0.92

Cost of entering the trade and maximum risk/share= 6.3-.92=5.38

Maximum profit/share= 15-5.38= 9.62

This gives us a reward risk of $1.78, which isn't all that great, to be honest. As you can see the vagaries of option pricing affect the profit and loss calculations quite a bit. In this case, due to the existing sentiment on AAPL, perhaps the far month calls are priced lower than the near month.

I've assumed a bullish condition but this is not reflected in the prices as you can see. In reality, the far month prices, in a bullish trend, will have higher prices and it is worthwhile for you to check them out as well if you're confident of the trend in the near term.

Considerations

Given the lack of a long stock position, your margin up front is a lot less on the bull call spread. Also, since the risk is defined by the premium you pay up front, figuring out the number of contracts you wish to carry is pretty straight forward. Simply figure out how much percent of your account the max risk is and make sure it is a low enough number that won't hit your account too hard in case the trade goes south.

Of course, bullish conditions are the primary underlying factor in the trade. If the market is wildly bullish, then there's no point in executing this since you'll only be limiting your gains. However, a volatile market, which is seeing a lot of counter-trend activity, provides an excellent set of conditions for you to deploy this strategy in.

Use technical indicators to determine the short-term direction and deploy this strategy wisely. I'll be covering technical indicators in a later section, so don't worry about this for now.

Bear Call Spreads

Bear or short call spreads are a trade which have an inverted reward risk profile but an extremely high success rate, assuming everything is executed well. This a strategy that a lot of professionals love, thanks to it being a steady income earner. However, risk management is absolutely critical since the potential loss you could incur is many multiples of the amount of money you stand to make.

This is a strategy where money keeps flowing in with small wins but execute something wrong and one loss will wipe everything away. A lot of beginners experience this due to getting complacent after the steady stream of money coming in.

This strategy is for sideways markets which are at a resistance zone or bearish markets. While selling a call is the best way to take advantage of a bear market, it is unlikely your broker will allow you to do this right off the bat. Hence, the bear call spread is an excellent strategy to deploy in such times.

How it Works

With a bear call spread, you will be writing an at the money or slightly out of the money call and buying a well out of the money option. Thus, on entering the trade, you will receive the premium from the lower strike price call and pay the lesser premium of the higher strike price call.

This is also the amount of your maximum profit on the trade. If the underlying stock increases in price beyond the first call, you will need to exercise your higher strike price call to buy the shares to fulfill the lower call being exercised. Thus, it is vital that your strike prices are close together and not too far apart, or else your trade will be stuck in a no man's land.

All of this is better illustrated via an example. AAPL is currently trading at $173.30 and the closest at the money call is $175, priced at $4.75. Now, let's assume $175 is a major resistance and that the stock is certain to turn back downwards once it reaches here. We write a call at $175 and earn the $4.75 premium.

It is a good idea to buy calls which are two steps past the lower strike price level. At this point in time, the strike price that is two steps away is the $180 call, which can be bought for $2.84.

Cost of trade entry/maximum profit per share= Premium received from writing lower call- Premium paid to purchase higher call= 4.75- 2.84= $1.91/ share.

Maximum loss= Strike price of higher call- strike price of lower call-net premium received on trade entry= 180-175-1.91= $3.09/share.

As you can see, the reward risk is inverted with this

strategy. Now, the best-case scenario for this trade is for both options to expire out of the money. In that case, you don't need to bother exercising either one of them.

The no man's land scenario is if the lower call moves into the money but the higher call doesn't. In this case, you'll have to buy the shares yourself, physically, at whatever the market price is and deliver the shares thanks to the lower call being exercised.

The worst-case scenario is price moving past the higher call, in which case you'll need to exercise it and deliver it. You'll obviously eat the entire loss in this case. This is why it is very important to make sure the price is in a strong bear trend or is near a strong resistance from which it will turn downwards.

Given the risk of this strategy, I personally recommend beginners to stick to options which are in the current month, instead of trying to capture the time decay of near month options. The additional time risk is too much and most beginners will not be able to manage risk well enough to stomach such losses.

Considerations

Your biggest concern with the bear call spread is the risk. Sure, you could widen the gap between the lower and higher call but to do so, you must be completely certain that the probability of price rising beyond the lower call is low. As always, market conditions play a huge role and you must be aware of these at all times.

What if you happen to be wrong about your market premise? What if, instead of being bearish, it turns out that the market makes a bull move? Well, this is where the adjustment comes into play.

You could flip your bear spread into a bull spread or, in the case of an expected bull market turning bearish, you could turn a bull spread into a bearish one. As always, the call levels are important. Needless to say, you need to buy and sell the same number of contracts and both legs of the trade must belong to the same calendar month.

Don't get fancy and try to arbitrage different months or make a volatility play. If you don't know what that sentence meant then don't worry. It was aimed at those traders who know just enough to trip themselves up.

Stick to the basics of these strategies and you'll find yourself making money consistently. If you are wondering if it's possible to successfully leverage calls with different month expiry dates, then yes, it is possible. This is what the calendar spread trade is all about.

Calendar Call Spreads

What if a stock is moving in an uptrend but is sluggish? There are many instances where the longer or medium term trend for a stock is bullish but in the short term, the market is going through a lot of counter-trend, bearish action. Once this action settles, it is clear that the stock will rise.

Well, this sort of scenario is what the calendar spread looks to take advantage of. Done right, you end up taking advantage of both the short term and long-term moves. This sort of flexibility is almost impossible on a directional trade and is a great reason as to why options strategies should be a part of every trader's arsenal.

What it is

A sluggish bull move is the perfect scenario for the calendar call spread. The premise is this: in the short term, the price is unlikely to move past a certain point but in the long term it certainly will. Thus, by writing the current month call for that strike price and by buying the near month call for the same strike price, we take advantage of both sides of the move.

The important thing to remember is that the strike price needs to remain the same. Without this, there's no real reasoning behind carrying out the trade. On paper, the calendar call achieves the exact same result as the covered call but for far less risk. Thus, the reward profile of this strategy is more attractive. Allied to this fact is the far lesser capital requirement this calls for and you have a perfect strategy for those middle of the road situations the market often finds itself in.

The first step is to determine the ideal strike price. This is where technical analysis really helps, especially support and resistance methods. I'll go over these in great detail later so you'll be able to determine not only the short term and long-term trend but also the best support and resistance levels.

Sticking to our favorite stock AAPL, let's say we determine that $180 is an ideal strike price. This is because AAPL is stuck under a short-term resistance at $175 and currently trading at $173.30. The $180 call is selling for $1.22. Mind you, this is the nearest term call option.

Looking at the near month, the $180 call is selling for $3.50. Thus our entry cost for this trade is:

Entry cost and maximum risk per share= Premium paid for near month call- Premium received for current month call= 3.5-1.22= $2.28 per share

The reward, in this case, is not capped since if the stock rises and places the longer-term call in the money, you can exit at whatever price you wish. In fact, you could exercise your option and turn it into a

65

profitable covered call strategy, as long as you maintain your bullish outlook.

The ideal scenario for such a trade is the current month call expiring out of the money and the longer term, near month call moving into the money. Even if the stock price doesn't move into the money, your risk is capped at the cost of entry.

Considerations

Determining the ideal strike price is the key to having success with this strategy. As mentioned, a good knowledge of technical analysis and S/R techniques will give you a massive edge in this regard. If you're neutral in the market or if the market seems to be stuck in a long range, choosing a slightly out of the money price is ideal. For more bullish environments, you will need to move out of the money as the rate of bullishness increases.

The calendar spread, when it works is a wonderful trade since you can parlay it into a covered call strategy by exercising the near month option. This way you can benefit from the bullish nature of the market and earn an income on your stock holding, reducing your cost basis the whole way.

Before diving into the trade, ensure the maximum risk amount is in line with your account's overall size. In other words, don't risk a large amount of your account. For beginners, this should be firmly under two percent of the overall account equity. Once you run a few trades yourself, you'll develop a better feel for which strike price works best.

This concludes our look at call spread trades. As you have seen, call spreads can be parlayed into three excellent strategies; the bull spread, the bear spread, and the calendar spread. Remember to always mark your maximum risk before entering the trade and be very clear as to what your exit scenario is, as described in the previous chapter on risk management.

There are a number of online options calculators which will do the numerical legwork for you if this isn't to your taste. Managing your risk is paramount with all strategies. This includes knowing what sort of an environment you're going into when applying the strategies in this book.

So always start with that first and then work your way down to which strategy you wish to deploy.

Chapter 7: Put Spreads

Much like how you can take advantage of call spreads, you can do the same with put spreads. Again, none of the following strategies call for underlying stock ownership and thus, the risk, as well as the margin required to establish a position, is greatly reduced.

A number of these spread trades can be converted into a collar under suitable situations. As we move forward, keep this in mind since it isn't always possible to list out every single exit scenario. Keep in mind the conditions required for a successful collar trade and after reviewing the strategies in this and the previous chapter, try to see how you could turn them into profitable collars.

As always, these strategies will make you money in bullish, bearish, and neutral market environments.

Bear Put Spread

The bear put spread is a strategy that will serve you well in bearish markets. Needless to say, you must avoid this in bullish or even neutral markets. Determining the course of the market or a stock is down to your technical analysis skills, which will be covered in detail later in the book.

For now, understand the basics of how this strategy works. All spread trades have the same underlying principles to them and thus, grasping one usually means you end up understanding the lot of them.

How it Works

The bear put involves selling an out of the money put and buying an at the money put. In a bearish market, the reasoning here is that once the stock declines you get to benefit from the increased price of the long-put position, which has a higher strike price and you earn the premium on the lower strike price put which you write.

In case price dives below the lower put, which puts it in the money, you will need to buy back the stock at the lower put strike price, since the option will be exercised. However, this is perfectly fine since you can exercise the higher strike price put that you've bought and clear a profit. The worst-case scenario is if price rises beyond the higher strike price put. In that case, the put that you wrote will limit your losses a bit thanks to the premium you receive on selling it.

The first step is to buy the higher strike price put. As usual, we'll be sticking to AAPL for our option chain prices. Currently, AAPL is trading at $176.06. Given the time decay effect, it is best to consider near month options since this gives the trade more space to breathe.

The closest out of the money put given this price is the $177 put which is selling at a premium of $5.95. For our out of the money put sale, let us sell the $150 put which is selling at $0.49. Now, we work out our maximum risk and profit numbers:

Maximum risk and cost of entering the trade per share= Premium paid for the higher strike price put- Premium received for the lower strike price put= 5.95-.49= $5.46 per share.

Maximum gain= Strike price of long put- strike price of short put- cost of trade entry= 177- 150- 5.46= $21.54 per share.

As you can see this is a fantastic reward risk profile. Given that each option contract holds one hundred shares, we're looking at a maximum reward of $2154 per contract for a risk of just $546 which is almost a 4x multiple. The key of course, is to check whether the risk amount is within your limits.

Considerations

The most obvious thing to look at is the market situation which should be heavily bearish. You might consider shorting the stock directly if the market is very heavily bearish. However, as mentioned in the respective section on call spreads, the market very rarely trends in a direction decisively. Most of the time, it's a mixture of with and counter-trend forces.

Thus, this strategy gives you the flexibility to enter position even when you aren't fully sure with how much force the market is going to decline.

The other thing to consider is the risk you're willing to carry. Obviously the further out of the money you go, the more your reward potential is. However, there's also the chance that the stock might not make it that far. A good idea in such scenarios is to measure the volatility of the stock in its preceding movement and to then estimate a price level which is within one and a half standard deviations out of the money.

This way, your lower strike price put is likely to stay out of the money so you'll earn the premium, while your higher price put increases in price. This is more of an art than science since it involves technical analysis but, for beginners, I recommend playing around with strike prices risking very little amounts.

The key to success with all spread strategies is to get used to the volatility of the underlying stock. Once you develop a feel for this, you won't really need the help of indicators to get an idea for what is a 'likely' price the stock will hit within a month or so, assuming normal market conditions.

As always, stay away from employing this strategy when events or announcements are expected. The spike in volatility will throw things off balance massively.

71

Bull Put Spread

A cousin of the bear put spread, the bull put requires a moderately bullish, or sideways, ranging market to be successful. Again, technical analysis will help you figure this out so make sure you digest the relevant chapter in this book thoroughly. With this strategy, as well as all spread strategies, the time decay is a very relevant part of your profits as targeting the near month options is a good idea.

You don't need to establish a long stock position with this strategy. Instead, this trade has two legs to it, a short and a long put with the same expiration date. Given the bearish nature of this strategy, it is the short put premium that will be your profit. This strategy works wonders over the longer term with LEAPS as well, thanks to the tax breaks you'll receive with a long term holding.

How it Works

Given the premise of a bullish market environment, price should be somewhere at or near a support level. The idea is to sell puts below this level since theoretically price should not make it past this. You can buy an out of the money put with a strike price a few levels below your first put in case price does break down through the support.

The further away the two puts are the greater your profits are. The idea is that the premium you receive from selling the higher priced put will pay for the premium of the lower priced one and if the price remains above support, you clear a profit right off the bat when you enter the trade.

Your first step is to determine which strike price to sell a put at. Let's stick with our AAPL example which is currently selling at $179.64. The closest at the money put is the $180 near month which has a premium of $5.70. Remember, we're assuming that the $180 level is a strong support and that price is not going to go below this.

Next, we need to find a lower strike price put to complete the second leg of the trade. Given that the timeline is a month, the $160 put seems a good choice. The premium for this is $1.10. So, we have the following numbers for this trade:

Cost of entry/Maximum reward per share= Premium received from writing higher priced put- Premium paid for lower priced put= 5.7- 1.1= $4.60 per share.

Maximum risk/loss= Strike price of higher put - Strike price of lower put - cost to enter= 180-160-4.6= $15.40 per share.

Now, the reward risk is badly skewed in this case, but this is mitigated by the overall bearish environment of the market and stock in question. Thus, it is essential for you to have a cogent market view before you enter such a trade.

Considerations

Aside from the bear market conditions, you should also be aware that your broker will require you to have substantial margin in your account for all strategies, including this one, which have skewed reward risk profiles. The reason for this should be obvious, given the higher potential risk the broker is exposed to.

For this particular trade strategy, you could adjust it to a bull put spread if things go pear-shaped. This is not an ideal scenario and you will need to take a call whether you wish to take a loss on the trade or convert. As always, risking the correct amount on your trades will make this decision easier for you.

By risking less, you won't feel compelled to make the money back in case things go against you. So always keep an eye on your risk management and consistently risk the same account percentage every single trade. In this case, the maximum loss should be within your per trade risk limit as discussed in the risk management chapter.

The worst-case scenario for this trade is if it dives below the second put, bringing both puts into the money. In this case, you will have to purchase the stock at the level of the higher put and sell it at the level of the lower put to mitigate your loss. You could hang onto it if you think your bearish view was in error and that a bullish revival is due. However, this is unlikely to be the case if you employed proper S/R techniques in the first place.

You must understand that trades will go wrong from time to time and that you will not win every single trade you take. This is why it is essential for you to define your exit points before even entering the trade and make sure you stick to it. This is just prudent risk management really. If you let your discipline fail in this regard, then your losses will wipe out all your gains, especially in skewed strategies like this one.

Just like with calls, puts can also be deployed in a calendar spread. Let's now take a look at this.

Calendar Put Spread

The calendar spread on puts works the same way as it does with the call calendar spread. Generally, the call spread is utilized more than the put, unless there is a greater than expected decline in the market or the put spread gives a greater return than the call spread.

This is a market neutral strategy and is excellent for sideways markets. Like with the call spread, the aim with this strategy is to sell the shorter term put and earn the premium while going long on the longer term put.

How it Works

The trade has two legs to it: the short term put and the long term put. The first step is to identify a suitable short term put to write. Generally, if the price is near a support level and you're expecting it to meander a bit before declining in the longer term, you can choose an at the money or slightly out of the money option.

The exact strike price you choose depends on the distance between the current price and the support level ahead. If there is a gap, choose a strike price that is beyond the support level. Sticking with our example of AAPL, let's assume it is at a support level which is going to hold for the short term before folding in the medium term.

Currently, AAPL is trading at $181.30 so let's assume $180 is our support level for the short term. The current month $180 put is the most suitable to write and doing this will fetch us a premium of $3.40. The near month $180 put will cost $5.95 to go long on and thus, our entry cost of the trade works out to:

Cost of trade entry/ Maximum loss per share= Premium paid for near month put- Premium received for current month put= 5.95-3.4= $2.55 per share.

The maximum reward, just like the call calendar spread, is something that depends on whether or not the stock falls below the support level over the medium term. If it does, you could exercise your near month option and ride the stock as it declines. Alternatively, you could trade the option itself and save yourself the commissions that arise from exercising it.

Considerations

The factors to take into account for this strategy are much the same as the call calendar spread, except this is a bearish version of that strategy. You want to identify a level that price is likely to remain above for the short term but will dip below during the medium term.

The reward risk profile of this trade is excellent and under the right market conditions, the calendar spread is a great strategy to deploy.

This also concludes our look at the put spread trades. Understandably, this chapter is shorter than the call spread trades chapter due to the principles governing the strategies remaining the same. Spread strategies are designed to take advantage of all kinds of markets.

It might seem on the surface that a lot of the strategies replicate one another but their individual risk profiles are different. So make sure you work out the numbers prior to entering them or deciding which one is better. Generally speaking, you can follow the below guidelines to help you decide.

When calls become expensive, as in the case of a bull

market on its last legs, bull call spreads work best. This is to capture whatever moderate level of gains there might be left. Of course, this presumes that you can read the decreasing strength of a trend well enough to deploy it in the first place.

In the final stages of a bear market, when volatility spikes and there aren't too many downside gains to be had, a bear call spread works best. Bear markets tend to be shorter than bullish ones since the general public doesn't indulge in the short side. Thus, bear markets don't suffer from the over-enthusiasm that tends to push bull markets for longer than expected.

The bull put spread works like a charm in a sideways market when you are certain that the overall trend is still bullish but currently, the stock is moving sideways or suffering from a bout of counter-trend enthusiasm. This is a good way to earn some income in the meantime and is a far safer option than trying to time a directional entry.

When a bear trend is accelerating to the downside, a bear put spread works the best. You could use this to hedge your positions in a long market but that's not a trading strategy per se. As it is, using it in the manner described previously is your best bet of making some money off it.

These spreads that I've described in this and the previous chapter are termed vertical spreads, with the exception of the calendar spread, which is a horizontal one. The term comes from the way in which option chains are displayed. The strike prices are listed vertically with the puts and calls arranged on either side of them. Thus, the lower strike price is above the current price and the higher ones below.

So by employing two legs on the trade, you're creating a vertical spread, as per the option chain table. With a calendar spread, you're on the same strike price, but visualizing a calendar, you're moving sideways or horizontally to the next month. Hence, the term horizontal spread.

You also would have noticed how some strategies, upon entry, pay you and some require an upfront cost. The ones that pay you are called net credit strategies and the ones that have a cost are called net debit ones. Net credit strategies pay you your maximum reward upfront, while net debit ones require you to wait for the maximum reward.

Of course, the flip side is that net debit strategies have you experiencing your full loss upfront, as opposed to net credit ones, where you need to see how it plays out. Take care to not develop a mental bias towards either one. All that matters is the market condition, not which one pays you first or last.

Chapter 8: Combinations

As great as spread trades are, a serious drawback to them is that the rewards they pay are limited compared to normal, directional strategies. While some spreads cap your maximum reward right off the bat, the ones that require you to wait also tend to produce comparatively limited rewards.

Now, I'm not advocating or saying that spread trades are bad or inefficient, far from it. It's just that options can be used to turbocharge your returns much like directional trades do. This is why combination trades are so powerful. Combination trades, in a few cases, do require you to commit to a certain market direction so they aren't all neutral like spread trades are.

However, your cost on entry into the trade is far lower than a directional bet and thus, you can use more of your leverage, provided your risk management is on point.

Combination trades are classified as either straddles or strangles. In this chapter, I'm going to break both of these strategies down so you'll be able to deploy these with ease when you're done reading this.

Straddles

The long straddle is a combination trade where you're not particularly invested in either side of the market. Whether the trend is bullish or bearish is of no concern. The only thing to avoid is a sideways market. As long as there is some sort of direction to the market, you only care about the degree or force with which the market moves in that direction.

The trade itself has two legs but both legs will be long positions. One of the legs is a long call and the other is long put. Both options will have the same expiry date, same month, and the same strike price. Needless to say, the quantity purchased of each should also be the same.

How it Works

The long straddle is a very simple trade to put into play. First, you buy an at the money call and then an at the money put. The idea is that one leg of the trade will rise in value depending on the direction the market takes. As the market moves in a direction, you could exit the unprofitable leg of the trade or hold onto it until expiry.

Meanwhile, the other leg of the trade will gain in value. The only thing to be careful of is that you will have moved your break-even point by the value you paid for the unprofitable leg. Thus, you want the profitable leg to move at least by that much. Thus, the key to success with this strategy is determining the probability of a big move in either direction in a stock.

Now, you could use technical analysis on the price chart for this but a much better way of doing this is to look at the implied volatility. Implied vol is an input which goes into the pricing of the option and the greater this number is the more the price of the option. Your key to success is to apply technical analysis principles to the chart of the implied vol and not the price chart.

In case you're a bit confused as to what the term means in the first place, let's take a step back. Volatility is the degree with which a stock moves in a given direction. The VIX, which is a popular chart, is a chart depicting the current volatility of the overall market. You need not concern yourself with how volatility numbers are calculated since this would be more appropriate for an advanced audience.

Instead, focus on when greater volatility occurs within stocks. Earnings announcements are a great example of this. Some companies have heavily anticipated earnings announcements and overperformance or underperformance in this regard often sends the stock rocketing in either direction. Election results also tend to have this effect on the overall market.

Important regulatory announcements also tend to

produce a lot of volatility in stocks as do announcements with regards to lawsuit outcomes. Tracking these basic fundamental factors in the news will narrow down your field of potential stocks in a jiffy.

As volatility increases, post announcement, the price of the option on the winning side of the trade increase dramatically, far more than the value you paid for the losing side. Thus, you don't have to worry about being right, as with a directional trade, you just need to make sure you're right to the correct degree.

A number of option trading platforms provide implied vol charts. Implied vol is simply the projection of volatility but this is plotted as a function of current time. For our purposes, you can regard volatility and implied vol as the same thing, despite there being some differences. As I said earlier, the differences are relevant for a more advanced audience.

A good source of free implied vol charts is www.alphaquery.com in case your broker belongs to the stone age. You can use this source until you find yourself a more suitable broker with a better platform. Do note, that the calls and the puts have their own implied vol values. These values are then averaged and the mean implied vol is plotted. It is this mean number you ought to focus on.

So what are some of the things to look for on the implied vol chart? Well, a dip to historic lows is a good bet. If the dip is hitting an important, prior historic low, you can bet that traders will pick up on this and there will be a bounce. Implementing a long straddle as the vol reaches this level is a good strategy.

Generally speaking, support and resistance techniques which you would use on a price chart apply equally as well on here. I wouldn't go so far as to use indicators and price patterns since that's just overkill.

The steps to implement the strategy are pretty straight forward. You buy the closest at the money call and at the money put and then watch for the market to move in either direction. If your volatility readings are correct, you'll find that one leg increases in price far beyond what it cost you to buy the unprofitable leg.

Continuing with the AAPL example, the closest at the money strike price currently is $180. The call will cost $6 to buy and the put will cost $5.95 to buy. Thus your entry cost is:

Trade entry cost and maximum risk per share= cost of call + cost of put = 6+5.95= $11.95 per share.

Your breakeven point to the upside is the strike price plus the put premium. Your break even to the downside is the strike price minus the call premium:

Break-even point to the upside= Call/put strike price + Put premium paid= 180+5.95= $185.95 per share.

Break-even point to the downside= Call/put strike

price - Call premium paid= 180- 6= $174 per share.

So to make a profit on the long leg of the trade, the call needs to move at least 5.95 points and, on the downside, the put needs to move at least 6 points. The worst-case scenario for the trade is if the stock remains in the band between $174 and $185.95, implying a sideways market.

Considerations

Deciphering whether the market is about to enter a range or continue on a trend is of the biggest concern with this strategy. While you can check implied vol to determine this, there is the question of timing. The market may remain in a low implied vol situation for longer than you might have bargained for.

The question of time brings forth another important point. With straddles, it is important you give the trade some time to play out. Thus, you should not employ this with current month options, unless there is some extremely important event that will occur in that period.

Near month or far month options work the best and give you the added advantage of having time decay on your side. Should you exit your unprofitable leg or should you take the entire loss? Well, this depends on how you approach your trade management. Certainly, letting the unprofitable leg expire worthless is suited for those who wish to adopt a bare minimum approach to the market but it does cost you more.

More active management is a better option but keep in mind that the activity required here is far less than what would be necessary for a regular directional trade. Generally speaking, if the price has cleared an important S/R level in whichever direction it has moved in, or if it has started a new leg of a trend, then you can safely close out the unprofitable leg.

This has the added effect of reducing your breakeven cost as well so let the profitable leg run for as long as possible. Make sure you close out your profitable position and don't let it expire by mistake! You can either exercise the option prior to expiry or you could sell the option itself. Either choice is a good one.

If the call happens to be your winning leg, you could parlay this into a covered call strategy. If the put happens to be a winner, your choices are less, but in some cases, a vertical spread might work. A collar could also be a good choice if you feel there is some consolidation ahead for the stock.

Thus, a straddle is an extremely profitable strategy when done right. The key is to begin with the implied vol and then figure out your unprofitable leg's exit points in order to reduce your break-even size. Either keep your winnings or translate this into another strategy to boost your earnings.

Strangles

Despite the rather gruesome-sounding name, strangles are a very popular and easy strategy to implement. As with straddles, you need not concern yourself with the direction of the market as much the degree with which it moves in the direction.

A strangle requires a lower up front investment but the flip side is that it demands a greater movement in the stock for it to realize any significant profit. The trade has two legs, similar to a straddle, with a long put and a long call. The only difference is that the strike prices of both are out of the money. Unlike the straddle, the strike prices are different.

How it Works

The first step is to determine which stocks in the market are due an explosive move soon. Such stocks will have historic lows of implied volatility, might be the target of takeovers or mergers, and other special events. The key difference between a straddle worthy stock and a strangle worthy one is the volatility is far far greater in the latter case.

With a strangle, we're looking for something that is going to move almost explosively in a given direction. Thus, the strategy has a lower success rate than a straddle but it compensates you with a higher than average win amount. Also, the cost to enter a strangle is far lower since you'll be dealing with out of the money options.

Looking over at AAPL, let's assume there's a huge announcement that is coming over the next few months, something like what the original iPhone launch was. Currently, the stock is trading at $179.50 but if the launch is successful, the stock price could shoot up to $220 and above. If unsuccessful, we can expect it to tank below $130.

Thus, we purchase a long put with a strike price of $150 and a long call with a strike price of $200. The former will cost us $0.51 and the latter costs us the same. Thus,

Cost of trade entry/ Maximum loss per share= Call premium paid + put premium paid = 0.51+0.51= $1.02 per share.

Your breakeven point is also not affected too much since it will move by just the premium cost of the losing leg. In this particular case, the stock needs to move 0.51$ past the strike price for you to break even. This is assuming you even hold on to the losing leg till expiry, instead of selling it before that.

If the move is explosive enough, you stand to make a decent profit, in far greater multiples of your risk.

Considerations

As you have probably realized by now, the band within which the trade realizes its worst-case scenario is a lot bigger than with a straddle. Thus, it is extremely important to screen the correct candidates prior to executing this strategy. More often than not, you'll find that the trade doesn't quite come off.

You can mitigate this by purchasing strike prices that are closer to the market price. From the above example, the $157.50 put can be purchased for $0.83 or about $30 more per contract. The $197.5 strike call can be had for $0.73, which is $20 more but isn't much of a reduction on the strike price.

Should the put and call be equidistant from the market price? Well, this is up to you. Some traders assume directionality by placing one of the legs closer to the market price. Thus, if your put is further away from the market than the call is to the market, you're probably assuming that a fall is more likely.

Get too close, of course, and you might as well use a straddle which will guarantee you money, even if it has a higher cost. There is no set quantitative rule with which you can determine a straddle versus strangle threshold, unfortunately. Like a lot of options trading, it is an art and a science.

You may have noticed that I've not addressed the short side of these strategies. This is because a short straddle and strangle involves selling an uncovered call and this is one of the riskiest things you can do. In fact, your broker will not allow it if you're just starting out so there really isn't any point going over these.

Briefly though, the short strategies work when you expect the market to remain in a range. While it is true that the market ranges more often than it trends, this doesn't automatically mean that the short straddles or strangles will work better. If you feel a range is forming, simply short the top boundary of the range and go long from the bottom using the stock.

This is the safest way to play a range and you don't need to worry about options in such scenarios. The point of using options is to leverage your money (without borrowing it) and reduce your risk. Using options to trade a range is doing the exact opposite.

This concludes our look at straddles and strangles, two wonderful strategies which can be used in times of volatility. The straddle costs more but is more likely to pay out. The strangle costs less but is less likely to pay out the huge amounts it promises. Implied vol is the key to both and look for higher, more explosive moves in the latter case.

Chapter 9: Market Environment

At this point, you have nine strategies to trade options for all kinds of market conditions, be it neutral, bearish, or bullish. While the strategies by themselves will limit your risk and give you rewards according to their risk profiles, the biggest risk in all of these is you applying the wrong strategy to the wrong market conditions.

There's no strategy that can completely eliminate the risk of you making a mistake, unfortunately. Even a neutral strategy, like the straddle or strangle, will not work if you misread a range for a trend.

Technical and fundamental analysis will help you determine what market conditions are appropriate. While every trader has different perspectives on this, personally, I tend to lean more towards technical analysis when it comes to determining which stocks to operate in. This is because fundamental analysis favors longer timelines, of over 5 years, for investment purposes. While the earnings announcements are important, a fundamentally low valuation doesn't play itself out over the course of a few months.

Thus, I'll be focusing mostly on technical analysis methods from here on out. Before we get to all of that though, you need to understand some basics about the market environment: namely, what is a trend and what is a range.

Trends and Ranges

The market is a chaotic place with a number of traders vying for dominance over one another. There are a countless number of strategies and time frames in play and at any point, it is close to impossible to determine who will emerge with the upper hand. In such an environment, how is it then possible to make any money? After all, if everything is unpredictable, how can you get your picks right?

Well, this is where thinking in terms of probabilities comes into play. While you cannot get every single bet right, as long as you get enough right and make enough money on those to offset your losses, you will make money in the long run. This goes back to what I spoke about in the risk management chapter.

It's not about getting one or two right. It's about executing the strategy with the best odds of winning over and over again, and ensuring that your math works out with regards to the relationship between your win rate and average win.

So it really comes down to finding patterns which repeat themselves over time in the markets. What causes these patterns? Well, the other traders of course! To put it more accurately, the orders that the other traders place in the market are what creates patterns that repeat themselves over time.

The first step to understanding these patterns is to understand what trends and ranges are. Identifying them and learning to spot when they transition into one another will give you a massive leg up not only with your options trading but also with directional trading.

Trends

In theory spotting a trend is simple enough. Look left to right and if the price is headed up or down, it's a trend. Well, sometimes it is really that simple. However, for the majority of the time you have both with and counter-trend forces operating in the market. It is possible to have long counter trend reactions within a larger trend and sometimes, depending on the time frame you're in, these counter-trend reactions take up the majority of your screen space.

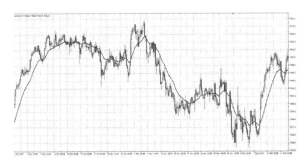

Figure 1: Trend vs Range

Take figure 1 for example. This is a chart of the UK100 CFD, which mimics the FTSE 100, on the four-hour time frame. Three-quarters of the chart is a downtrend and the last quarter is a wild uptrend. Using the looking left to right guideline, we'd conclude that this instrument is in a range. Is that really true though?

Just looking at that chart, you can clearly see that short-term momentum is bullish. So if you were considering taking a trade on this, would you implement a range strategy or a trending one? This is exactly the sort of thing that catches traders up.

The key to deciphering trends is to watch for two things: counter trend participation quality and turning points. Let's tackle counter trend participation first.

Counter Trend Participation

When a new trend begins, the market experiences extremely imbalanced order flow which is tilted towards one side. There's isn't much counter trend participation against this seeming tidal wave of with trend orders. Price marches on without any opposition and experiences only a few hiccups.

As time goes on though, the with trend forces run out of steam and have to take breaks to gather themselves. This is where counter trend traders start testing the trend and trying to see how far back into the trend they can go. While it is unrealistic to expect a full reversal at this point, the quality of the correction or pushback tells us a lot about the strength distribution between the with and counter-trend forces.

Eventually, the counter-trend players manage to push so far back against the trend that a stalemate results in the market. The with and counter-trend forces are equally balanced and thus the trend comes to an end. After all, you need an imbalance for the market to tip one way or another and a balanced order flow is only going to result in a sideways market.

While all this is going on behind the scenes, the price chart is what records the push and pull between these two forces. Using the price chart, we can not only anticipate when a trend is coming to an end but also how long it could potentially take before it does. This second factor, which helps us estimate the time it could take, is invaluable from an options perspective, especially if you're using a horizontal spread strategy.

Here's what you look out for to gauge counter trend participation:

1. Quality of counter-trend candles- Are they strong/weak/have wicks/small bodied, etc.?

2. Number of counter-trend candles within the movement- Is this changing over time?

3. Length of pushbacks- Are the pushbacks increasing in number? Are they lasting for longer?

In all cases, the greater the number of them, the greater the counter-trend participation in the market. The closer a trend is to ending, the greater the counter-trend participation. Thus, the minute you begin to see price move into a large, sideways move with an equal number of buyers and sellers in it, you can be sure that some form of redistribution is going on.

Mind you, the trend might continue or reverse. Either way, it doesn't matter. What matters is that you know the trend is weak and that now is probably not the time to be banking on trend strategies.

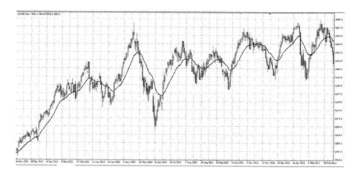

Figure 2: Counter Trend Participation

In figure 2, we can see how counter trend participation changes over time on the FTSE. Starting from the left, we can see that there is close to no counter trend bars, bearish in this case, and the bulls

96

make easy progress. Note the angle with which the bulls proceed upwards.

Then comes the first major correction and the counter-trend players push back against the last third of the bull move. Notice how strong the bearish bars are and note their character compared to the bullish bars.

The bulls recover and push the price higher at the original angle and without any bearish presence, which seems odd. This is soon explained as the bears slam price back down and for a while, it looks as if they've managed to form a V top reversal in the trend, which is an extremely rare occurrence.

The price action that follows is a more accurate reflection of the power in the market, with both bulls and bears sharing chunks of the order flow, with overall order flow in the bull's favor but only just. Price here is certainly in an uptrend but looking at the extent of the bearish pushbacks, perhaps we should be on our guard for a bearish reversal. After all order flow is looking pretty sideways at this point.

So how would we approach an options strategy with the chart in the state it is in at the extreme right? Well, for one, any strategy that requires an option beyond the near month is out of the question, given the probability of it turning. Secondly, looking at the order flow, it does seem to be following a channel, doesn't it?

While the channel isn't very clean, if you were

aggressive enough, you could consider deploying a collar with the strike prices above and below this channel to take advantage of the price movement. You could also employ some moderately bullish strategies as price approaches the bottom of this channel and figuring out the extent of the bull move is easier thanks to you being able to reference the top of the channel.

As price moves in this channel, it's all well and good. Eventually though, we know that the trend has to flip. How do we know when this happens?

Turning Points

As bulls and bears struggle over who gets to control the order flow, price swings up and down. In figure 2, we can see a number of swings where the bulls pushed the bears, and the price, back upwards to maintain the uptrend. You will notice that every time price comes back into the 6427-6349 zone, the bulls seem to step in en masse and repulse the bears.

This tells us that the bulls are willing to defend this level in large numbers and strongly at that. Given the number of times the bears have tested this level, we can safely assume that above this level, bullish strength is a bit weak. However, at this level, it is as if the bulls have retreated and are treating this as a sort of last resort, for the trend to be maintained. You can see where I'm going with this.

If this level were to be breached by the bears, it is a good bet that a large number of bulls will be taken out. In martial terms, the largest army of bulls has been marshaled at this level. If this force is defeated, it is unlikely that there's going to be too much resistance to the bears below this level.

This zone, in short, is a turning point. If price breaches this zone decisively, we can safely assume that the bears have moved in and control the majority if the order flow.

Figure 3: Turning Point Breached

Figure 3 shows us the eventual order flow as the trend turns. The decisive turning point zone is marked by the two horizontal lines and the price touches this level twice more and is repulsed by the bulls. Notice how the last bounce before the level breaks produces an extremely weak bullish bounce and price simply caves through this. Notice the strength with which the bears break through.

The FTSE was in a longer uptrend on the weekly chart so the bulls aren't completely done yet. However, as far as the daily timeframe is concerned, notice how price retests that same level but this time around, it acts as resistance instead of support. I'll talk more about this in the next chapter on S/R levels.

For now, we can conclude that as long as the price remains below the turning point, we are bearishly biased. Given the amount of bullish participation in figure 3, we can safely assume that the bear trend is going to get reversed soon as well. You can see this by looking at the angle with which bulls push back as well as, the lack of strong bearish participation on the push upwards.

This doesn't mean we go ahead and pencil in a bull move and start implementing strategies that take advantage of the upcoming bullish move. Remember, nothing is for certain in the markets. Don't change your bias or strategy until the turning point decisively breaks.

Some key things to note here are that a turning point is always a major S/R level. It is usually a swing point where a large number of with trend forces gather to support the trend. In figure 3, we have a situation where the turning point for the bull trend is the same as the one for the ensuing bear trend. This will not always be the case, so don't make the mistake of hanging on to older turning points.

The current order flow and price action are what matters the most, so pay attention to that above all else. We can safely designate the same level in figure 3 as the bearish turning point as well because of the fact that this level gets tested multiple times and each time, the bears repulse the bulls back down. Also, note how the candles that test this level all have wicks on top of them.

This indicates that the bears are quite strong here and that any subsequent attack will be handled the same way until the level breaks. Do we know when the level will break? Well, we can't say with any accuracy. However, we can estimate the probability of it breaking.

The latest upswing has seen very little bearish pushback, comparatively speaking, and the push into the level is strong. Instinct would say that there's one more rejection left here. However, who knows? Until the level breaks, we stay bearish. When the level breaks, we switch to the bullish side.

Putting it all Together

So now we're ready to put all of this together into one coherent package. Your analysis should always begin with determining the current state of the market. Ranges are pretty straightforward to spot and they occur either within big pullbacks in trends or at the end of trends.

Trends vary in strength depending on the amount of counter-trend participation they have. The way to determine counter trend participation levels is to simply look at the price bars and compare the counter-trend ones to the with trend ones. The angle with which the trend progresses is a great gauge as well, for its strength, with steeper angles being stronger.

Next, you need to determine the turning point of the trend. The turning point is a level that is extremely well defended by the with trend players and will be attacked repeatedly by the counter-trend traders in long trends. Determining a good turning is a question of reading the support and resistance well, which will be made clear in the next chapter.

Once you have the turning point figured out, you need to then stick to your bias and let the S/R guide you with regards to strike prices for your options strategies. Reading support and resistance is an essential skill you must master. So let's look at this in more detail.

Chapter 10: Support and Resistance

Support and resistance levels, on the surface, seem as simple to decipher as trends. After all, much like looking left to right, simply mark whichever level price has bounced from and that's it, right? Well, if it were that simple, trading would be the easiest thing in the world and there would be no need for books like this one.

This is not to say that S/R is complicated. Far from it. What trips up most traders is not their ability to spot levels but their mindset in locating them as we'll shortly see.

Order Flow Levels

Instead of designating the levels price bounces from as support and resistance, a more accurate term would be to call them order flow levels. This is because when viewed from an order flow perspective, it's a whole lot easier to understand which level is going to play an important role and why.

You see, the default method of S/R is to only look at

price levels in the past and ignore what it is doing currently. There's no taking into account the counter-trend distribution or the current bias of the market. All of these play a very important role in determining what is going to act as an S/R level in the near future, from where the price is going to have a reaction you can take advantage of.

How S/R is Formed

As price moves in a given direction, buyers and sellers interact and leave an imprint for everyone to see. In some cases, one side overwhelms the other and, in some cases, both sides reach a mutual agreement over a certain price point. There are some areas on the chart which are more suitable for such mutual agreement than others.

Why would traders agree on such price points? Well, the causes are numerous. Perhaps there was some fundamental event that took place or perhaps this number has some sort of psychological significance. Perhaps, some trader cornered the market and thought it would be funny. This doesn't happen anymore, thanks to the size of the stock market but every once in a while, you will see such shenanigans on the commodities markets. Such occurrences are more frequent than you might think on the bond markets.

Speaking of which, bond markets have an impact on

the stock market as well. The bond markets are entirely institutional and are about ten times the size of the stock market. A lot of hedge funds and banks place bets on the stock market via derivatives in the bond market and thus, the ripple effect is felt in stocks.

My point is this: No one knows why a level is important. It isn't your job to determine why a level is important. What you need to figure out is, which level do the largest number of traders think is important. Thus, the importance of a level is directly tied to the current order flow characteristics.

If the bears are heavily dominant, would they consider a level where they previously fought off the bulls important? Or would they consider a level where the bulls fought back earnestly as more important? There's no straightforward or formulaic answer to this. Much like with the rest of the market, all we have is probabilities.

The best we can do is identify patterns of support and resistance and see how traders treat prior price reaction points with respect to current order flow and project how they might react in the future. All of this sounds more complicated than it actually is. However, a point I'd like to emphasize here is that there's no gain in you defining set rules for yourself when it comes to S/R.

A lot of beginners come in with weird rules like "the prior swing high is not as important as the prior swing low in a bull trend retest" and so on. Well, every bull trend's order flow characteristics are different and there's no way we can know in advance or hypothetically how something will behave. The best way to form a decision is to look at a chart and draw conclusions based on what you see.

So let go of the rules or even your need for them. It is counter-intuitive but letting go of rules will actually result in your trading in a far more disciplined manner since you're now in line with the true nature of the market, which is to respect the odds and not seek certainty over every single thing.

Zones

The first lesson for you to learn is that price levels are not single horizontal lines like they're depicted in charts but zones. Remember, the market is made of traders placing orders. There are traders on your time frame, on time frames multiple levels below you, and above you. It's unrealistic to think that all these millions of traders will think of a single number as being the definitive support or resistance level. So when looking for S/R, look for zones, not simple horizontal lines.

The biggest indicator of a good S/R level is the amount of order flow it has seen. Indications of heavy order flow are multiple touches, prolonged testing of a level, and so on. The further away the tests of the level are from one another, the better. From an order flow perspective, this indicates that traders believe this level contains support for a given side of the market over time and this isn't just a short-term fad.

Figure 4: Strong S/R Zones

Figure 4 illustrates strong support and resistance zones simultaneously. This is a characteristic of ranges. The instrument is the FTSE 100 and the timeframe is the daily chart. Notice on the bottom, that after the initial double dips in August and mid-September (themselves a month apart), the price dips back into this level in mid-December and is still respected. In the new year, despite a strong bearish push into the bottom, the level still holds for a few days before breaking down.

On top, the hits are not as far apart as on the bottom but they're still numerous. October through November sees the FTSE constantly pushing against the top but without any success. Then, the December push up also gets rejected.

Figure 4 gives us a handy lesson on spotting good S/R levels in advance, so let's look at this chart moving left to right. First off, we have a very strong bear trend in place, which is evidenced by the strong bearish bars and the complete absence of bullish bars. Notice how the bearish bars increase in size as price dips.

Then the bulls astonishingly push back against this force. In what is a sign of the bear strength, despite three strong bullish bars, they run out of steam and price dips back down below. Now, here's the situation. We know that we're in a bearish trend. We also know there's a support level coming up where bulls pushed back against a very strong bear trend. How probable is it that this level is going to receive bullish support again?

Very probable, one would think. Given that the bearish pressure is nowhere near what it was on the initial dip, odds are that the bulls present at that level will be able to step in again and probably push the price higher this time. This is what happens in mid-September. Indeed, the bulls step in at a higher price level than before. The message to the bears is clear: this is a strongly defended level and it's going to take a lot of firepower to break through.

When price returns to this level in mid-December, it is a strong push down but is it as strong as the initial push down? Hardly. So odds are good that the bulls will hold this level again, and they promptly do.

However, the bounce they produce this time around is a lot lower than previously, only three quarters or so of the previous push up. This tells us that the bulls may be weakening.

Bears promptly push price back down and there's no bullish reaction to this push down prior to price reaching the level. We see that all the bulls can do is hold the price at this level but not push and eventually they exhaust themselves as the bears push through.

What does all this mean for your options strategies? Well, hopefully, it's clear to you what the range boundaries are and what your strike prices for range strategies ought to be. Secondly, as price reaches the support, this is a good time for you to employ some bullish strategies. Do you know when the range bottom will break? Well, maybe but you can't say with any great odds. So a horizontal spread is out.

Instead, any call or put strategy you employ can have its strike prices below the support level, given the inability of price to push past this. You can use the same tactics at the top of the range as well, although the top doesn't give multiple opportunities like the bottom does.

The best opportunity is the push upwards in late November where a clear strike price would be above the resistance boundary. Given the number of hits previously and the way the bears defended this level, the odds are good it will hold. Besides, the overall trend is bearish so perhaps a longer time horizon is warranted. This way, you can capture a greater portion of the time decay in your trade.

Generally speaking, the time you want your counter trend trades to run should be far lesser than your with trend trades. Is there a fixed template for you to follow? Well, again, it's not that simple. As the range grows older you should expect the odds of it breaking down to increase so you should shorten your time horizon accordingly. The last trade off the bottom, for example, would have not run till expiration. Some trial and error, in other words experience, is needed to really nail this.

Keep your risk per trade low at the start and as you gain experience, you'll figure out how long to let your trades run. Even better, hedge your directional option bets with neutral strategies like straddles and strangles or simple strategies like the collar. This way you can literally earn while you learn.

Tips

There are some easy to spot characteristics of potentially good S/R levels. I've already mentioned how you need to focus on the order flow characteristics in order to figure out which levels will be relevant to the current situation. A good place to start is by looking at prior swing points.

Swing points are tricky things to deal with since the

level of current order flow imbalance dictates whether the prior swing point will be respected or not. If the order flow at prior swing point wasn't terribly significant, you can expect an imbalanced current order flow to plummet through it without pause. That was a mouthful to type and understand so it's best we look at an example of this.

Figure 5: S/R Levels

Figure 5 is the FTSE once more, this time in an uptrend. We can see two swing lows which are indicated by the horizontal lines. The bottom low is more of a zone and is denoted by two horizontal lines. The upper swing low is marked by a single line since the price didn't really hang around here for too long before going on upwards.

Now, as price retraces its way back to the original level, how do we determine whether this level will hold or not? Well, we start with the current order flow. Before the first bearish bar into the level, we have the odd scenario of price gapping down on open but still ending up bullish for the day. This is not something you'll see very often and to be honest it can be hard to know what to make of this. Let's reserve judgment for now.

The bearish bar into the level clarifies things immensely though. Not only is it far bigger than the previous bearish bars, it comes on the back of bearish pressure previously seen. This is also the biggest bar printed for a long time now. So, we know that order flow is tilted towards the bears. Now, let's look at the potential support which is our upper swing point.

Was the bearish pressure into this level strong? Hardly. Was this a level the bulls had to mount a lot of force into in order to defend. Given the lackluster bearish attack on it, this doesn't seem to be the case. Thus, we can conclude that this level probably doesn't have much significant bullish presence and we can ignore this level as of the current moment. On a live chart, you need not even mark this level since it is insignificant.

The swing point below is a different matter. While the bearish reaction here was not particularly strong, it was a place where the bears mounted some resistance to pretty steep bullish pressure (look at the angle of the upswing going into the level). Against this sort of bullish pressure, the bears were strong enough to keep the price at this level for quite some time and even dampen the slope of the upswing. Clearly, the bearish pressure was significant here.

The fact that the bulls overcame this is quite significant. Thus, despite the strong bearish pressure into the lower swing point's level, we can say that the odds of this level holding appear to be good. Do we know for certain that it will hold? No. However, the odds are good and that's all we need. Turns out that in this case, we were correct but it is possible to be wrong as well, of course, despite the evidence we've seen.

Another key tip for identifying strong S/R levels is to check whether the level is present on a higher time frame. Often, you'll see price form a V top or bottom in a given time frame and this can appear confounding until you go up one level and see that it did this because it bounced off a higher time frame level.

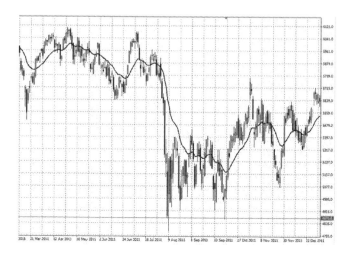

Figure 6: FTSE Daily Bounce

Figure 6 shows a steep downtrend on the FTSE after a range. Initially, this downward swing looks apocalyptic. However, around 4870, price violently bounces back up and the FTSE reverses course as if nothing happened. Not only that, it doesn't even reapproach it after an initial retest. It's like all that bearish pressure was pointless. What gives?

Well, figure 7 holds the answer. I've marked the level more accurately in this figure and the bounce on the daily is the second bounce on the right-hand side of figure 7. As you can see, the price was headed smack into a very strong level on the weekly chart which had been defended by the bulls previously.

If anything, the current push into the level was mild compared to the previous violent push into this level, as we can see by the tail that is formed on the bearish

114

weekly bar in the first swing point. Seen in this context, the daily bearish push seems rather meek. If you were aware of this level beforehand, you could have executed a bullish directional strategy with your strike prices beyond the support zone. Odds are with the bearish pressure headed into it, you would have received a good deal on the premiums as well.

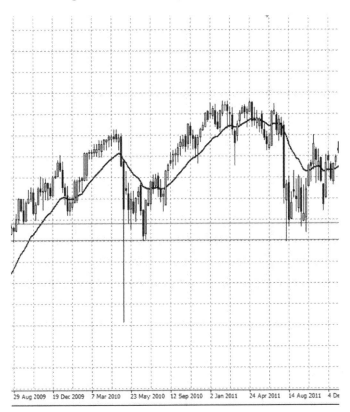

Figure 7: FTSE Weekly Bounce

The key to mastering S/R is to practice, a lot. Your success with options strategies depends on you understanding S/R and trends vs ranges more than understanding the deep intricacies of a vertical spread. Follow the key points as mentioned in this chapter and you'll do just fine.

To summarize, here they are:

1. Prior swing points are good places to start looking for possible S/R.

2. Prior order flow points where there was significant bullish or bearish pressure are good places to start as well.

3. Order flow and bias into the level matter. Stronger the imbalance, the stronger the level needs to be to hold price.

4. Higher time frame S/R points are always significant, irrespective of the lower time frame order flow imbalance. This doesn't mean they'll always hold, just that you can expect the price to hiccup at it at the very least.

Chapter 11: Fundamentals and Sentiment

While technical analysis should form the backbone of your analysis strategy, it can hardly be a starting point for screening stocks. You could either reduce your watchlist to a small handful of stocks and observe them for opportunities or you could cast a wider net and nitpick the most promising ones.

Both approaches have advantages and disadvantages. By reducing the size of your watchlist, you will familiarize yourself with your chosen instruments to a greater degree and will be in a better position to take advantage of any opportunity. However, the opportunities may be few and far in between. You could also end up choosing stocks which simply don't move as much with the rest of the market and miss a number of moves.

By screening stocks, you won't face this problem since you'll be able to cherry-pick the ones with the best potential. The downside is that the constant chopping and changing of your trading instruments will lead to you not having a good picture of the instrument's volatility. Thus, you won't be fully in sync with the size of the stock's usual support and resistance zones and you might end up placing your strike prices in the wrong locations, thereby invalidating your trades.

So what should you do? For beginners, I recommend combining the two approaches by following a strict screening process with a trading period of a few months. Running the screen after some time in order to refresh the watchlist will ensure you still remain up to date with the larger market by exposing yourself to new stocks as well as gaining experience by trading the same instruments over and over.

There are many methods of screening stocks. However, for the purposes of trading options, we need to stick to just a few fundamental and sentimental factors to narrow our options down. This chapter will give you this framework and you're free to either expand or narrow it down further.

Fundamentals

Traditional fundamental analysis focuses on things like the earnings, the dividend payout ratio and a host of other metrics like EBITDA and free cash flow. Are any of these relevant from a speculative trading perspective? Well, they're not irrelevant. However, it would be quite a stretch to call any of these really relevant to your trading performance.

The fundamentals you have to keep your eye on are more general in nature such as the overall economic condition and the state of particular sectors in the market. While you need not know the ins and outs of it, you should be able to form a decent answer to questions like 'will lower interest rates benefit the infra sector or hurt it' and so on. Again, you don't need to write a long thesis on it, just a simple one-word answer will do. You need not even be right, as long as you just know that there is a relationship there, you'll be fine.

You should stay on top of economic releases. It's a good idea to read these releases and the analysis of them just to get a better view of things. It won't inform your trading decisions but it will help you get up to speed on the lingo. A lot of beginners fall for the Hollywood effect which shows traders as a bunch of maniacs who track economic releases and make billions of them.

You will not be doing any such thing so relax. If this disappoints you then you perhaps need to pick a more exciting field of work. Trading is, contrary to most expectations, quite boring as a profession. Most of the time, you'll just be sitting around reading stuff.

Anyway, you should be aware of economic announcements since they produce huge volatility spikes in the market. If you're trading a neutral strategy then these announcements are veritable gold mines since the degree of movement is huge. While the premiums will take into account the additional volatility, you can still clear a large amount.

Economic Releases and General Market Conditions

Announcements like interest rates, conferences like the annual Fed meet at Jackson Hole and the NFP are the major economic releases you need to be aware of. Press conferences and statements from the leading government officials also sway markets. They're generally quite a responsible lot and all of their statements and press conferences are scheduled ahead of time in a manner so as to reduce market disruption.

There's, of course, an odd loose cannon, none more so than the President and his twitter account these days, but everyone seems to have figured out he's not a great source of information so the impact of his tweets are not as great as one would imagine.

You should also be aware of general market levels and conditions. Keeping the important support and resistance levels in mind is a good idea. Of course, if you choose to trade the SPX options, this problem is solved for you. The most important thing for you to know about the general market is the current trend/range situation.

Is the market bullish, bearish or in a range? What is the distribution of order flow? Where are the turning points? I'll address why these are important shortly, but for now, remember to keep these in mind.

Stock Specific Factors

I know I haven't specified as yet how you narrow your focus down to specific stocks but will do so shortly. For now, keep in mind that you should be aware of any events taking place with your chosen stock. A great place to start is to scan the 10-K annual filings of the company. This lists all the current events, lawsuits, etc. that the company is facing and where things stand.

Potential takeovers and mergers are also great volatility producing events as are divestment decisions. Conglomerates often spin off their subsidiaries into smaller companies and the effect on the parent company's stock can be substantial, depending on how the market view it. Takeovers, whether they go through or fail are great for market neutral strategies.

Dividend increases or decreases produce spikes as well. Now, with the exception of takeovers and spinoffs, I'm not recommending you target any of these announcements with a strategy. Merely be aware that an announcement is on the horizon and that you can expect additional volatility. Know how this will affect your position.

You will find some experts recommending you drill through the annual reports and seek out companies which are expected to announce less than stellar earnings and take advantage of such announcements.

Frankly, this is a waste of time. If you're good enough to analyze companies well enough to determine which one is going down the toilet, you're better off spending your time finding good companies to invest in for long term investment purposes since that growth is unlimited.

This is why I'm not wasting time listing PEG and earnings ratios since they're irrelevant for speculative purposes and this is not a book on investment. Bottom line: be aware of the volatility spike these announcements produce and take this into account when you determine your strike prices. The exceptions are spinoffs and takeovers.

Sector Specific Factors

Each stock belongs to a particular sector. You should have a rough idea of what the talk is currently about that particular sector. If you're speculating with a defense contractor's stock for example, what is the talk currently and who is the US planning on bombing next, roughly speaking? The idea is to not be blind. Again, you don't need to be an expert, just know the outline.

The things you should be aware of, however, is the sector's technical performance. Much like you should know the market's current state and turning points, you should be aware of the sector's overall performance. A lot of brokers and charting software will allow you to chart the overall sector's performance, which is really just the composite of all the individual stocks in that sector.

Once you have this composite chart in front of you, you need to analyze it from an order distribution and turning points perspective and more importantly, see how the sector is performing relative to the market. If the market is bullish, has the sector kept pace with it or is it still sideways?

It's a good idea to map out all the major sectors in the market in this fashion and classify them as either par, weaker or stronger. The weaker ones are those which are not moving with the same force as the market and stronger ones are those which are rising faster than the market.

Here's the first step in narrowing down your list of stocks: In market bear trends, stick to the weaker sectors. In bull trends, stick to the stronger ones. In ranges, stick to the ones on par. The sectors which are weak will not always be so, you'll see a cycling of sectors between the categories. Simply switch sectors when this happens, as long as the overall market condition holds.

Much like you picked the stronger sectors in bull markets, pick the stronger stocks within the sectors to speculate with. That is, in bull markets pick those stocks which are stronger than the sector composite and the weaker ones in a bear market.

This way, you'll end up with a handful of stocks for every sector and this should form your main watchlist.

Sentiment Analysis

Sentiment analysis should augment your fundamental analysis. Market sentiment is simply a guide to what the overall emotion is within the market. There are strategies out there which take advantage of this but for the ones outlined in this book, you don't need to use sentiment as anything beyond an accessory to your trades.

A good example of using sentiment to inform your trades is if you have narrowed down which stock you wish to trade and review the sentiment currently within it to inform your decision. At most, the sentiment will affect your strike price levels but not invalidate your trade unless something is really off.

So what are the factors which inform market and stock specific sentiment?

VIX

The VIX is the flag bearer for all things volatility. It is an index which measures the current volatility of the stock market and generally is thought of as projecting the short term, monthly volatility expectation of stock market traders. The accuracy of the VIX is pretty spot on because it is derived from the implied volatility on the SPX options.

As market sentiment grows more and more bearish, the VIX tends to increase in value and the more bullish things are the lower the value of the VIX. For this reason, it has been termed the 'fear index' by many market observers since it approximates the amount of fear or uncertainty present amongst traders in the market.

So what does all this mean for you? Well, unless the VIX is at all-time highs or lows, you really shouldn't be too focused on whether your position is valid or not. It is possible to draw support and resistance levels on the VIX and try to time positions on that basis but this only works for the SPX.

For individual stocks, you just need to check up on its health and make sure you aren't going up against some historical levels. As for the SPX, you could try to time entries on the basis of S/R on the VIX. However, always let the environment and levels on the S&P guide you and have this augmented by the VIX instead of making volatility your sole entry factor.

As mentioned before, you can use the VIX for more complex strategies but these are not beginner appropriate and are out of scope for this book.

Put/Call Ratio

The put to call ratio is another fear indicator with the ratio being high during times of fear and being low when times are bullish or normal. Again, this ought to be just used as a check for the sanity of your position, so to speak. Your analysis of the individual price action should override everything else.

You can use the ratio as a screening tool to see whether there's any build up prior to an important support or resistance level. However, it's a good bet that every other trader in the market is using this as well so don't expect great results from it.

If your analysis tells you that a major fall is expected and the put-call ratio is pretty low, consider taking a directional position. This is because if you turn out to be right and the rest of the market is wrong, as evidenced by the low ratio, you could make a killing. So, in such times, you can use the ratio as a contrarian indicator.

Open Interest

Much like the put to call ratio, this number gains its power from being used as a contrarian indicator, especially to spot the end of trends. Open interest is the number of contracts that are available for trading. Volume is a measure of how much of these contracts are actually traded but OI is the best gauge of the appetite the market has for a particular side of the market.

In a bearish trend is you see a massive spike in the

number of puts being bought then this is your best indication that the trend is coming to an end soon. Allied with a technical review, such as the number of counter-trend traders increasing in number to the point where order flow is almost balanced, this can function as a signal to go the other way and change your bias.

I wouldn't recommend actually changing your bias until the turning point is breached, however. This is because you could see a spike in OI but it's not always possible to tell what a normal spike is versus an unjustified one. Just keep your eyes open for this and stay updated.

Much like the number of puts increase towards the end of a bear trend, you'll see a far greater spike at the end of a bull trend. These spikes are caused by the beginner traders and the general public finally getting into the market because their friendly financial TV show told them the market is going to rise or fall forever.

A lot of successful trading is simply figuring out what beginners or the uninformed would do and then doing the exact opposite.

Short Interest

This is the number of shorts placed on the stock and is to be used as a contrarian indicator solely. As the bearish trend intensifies more and more puts and shorts are placed and when this number spikes, you can be sure the clueless beginners are in. Combined with a technical observation, this is the best indication you can have for a reversal.

To clarify further, short interest is the measure of stock that has been shorted but not covered as yet in the market. You'll usually see this expressed as a percentage, indicating the amount of open order volume that is net short, or as a number which is simply the volume.

While short interest spikes do indicate reversals near the end of trends, it is an extremely useful indicator prior to trends beginning. The key is to figure out when high-quality orders are being placed to short the stock. In other words, whenever you see a spike in the short interest volume, you need to verify it from a market situation perspective.

If you see a spike when the price is at the end of a range, this indicates that price is probably going to break down below the bottom of it. The high-quality shorts are loading up and you ought to go along with them. This is especially useful because it tells you of a breakdown prior to it actually happening, something which is tough to decipher by just looking at the price bars in a range.

Contrast this with what happens at the end of a trend when lots of counter-trend interest is present and the smart with trend players are out of the market, having long since made their profits. A spike in short interest here indicates an influx of traders who are late getting on the bandwagon and will soon be squeezed.

This concludes our look at fundamental and sentimental factors. Use fundamentals to screen stocks as mentioned and keep your screens updated especially your composite sector charts. Build a list of stocks across all sectors and monitor these. After some time, maybe four or five months, update this list and observe again.

Remember to follow up all of this with technical analysis and S/R analysis of your chosen stocks. The only exception to this might be when you see a huge event coming up and, in that case, you can ignore the technicals and simply enter a straddle. However, this is not advisable, a technical review always pays dividends.

Conclusion

So here we are at the end of this book. We've now covered ten profitable options strategies you can use across all markets, including two powerful strategies you can use where you don't need to be concerned with which way the market will move. We've looked at strategies where you can generate steady income on an existing position, completely risk-free.

We've looked at how you can use calls and puts to generate income for you, irrespective of whether or not you need to buy the underlying stock. We've learned about horizontal and vertical spreads and collars. Along the way, you've also seen why options trading is the best way to reduce your risk and leverage your capital, without actually borrowing a cent.

Remember, that risk management is paramount. Always stick to your per trade risk figures and do not deviate from this no matter how attractive the setup might seem. Remember, the odds of success of a slam dunk looking setup and one that looks like a dog's dinner is exactly the same. The market doesn't care about how pretty your setup is so neither should you. As long as the underlying conditions are fulfilled, you should execute your setup in the correct manner.

Your analysis should always begin with the technical

market situation which is the order flow distribution and the trend or range situation. Often you will deal with trends with close to equal participation from both sides of the market. This should tell you that a reversal is probably imminent and you should adjust accordingly.

Support and resistance will play an important role in determining where you ought to place your strike prices. Remember to evaluate support and resistance levels from an order flow perspective, instead of looking at every single available level on the chart. Look at the order flow characteristics the previous time price made it there and compare it to the current order flow to get a feel for whether the level will hold or not.

Screening stocks is a straightforward matter if you follow the process outlined here. Compare the sector performance to the overall market performance to narrow down which sectors you ought to focus on. Once this is done, repeat the same process with individual stocks to select the best to speculate with.

It is a good idea to put all of this into a trading plan in order to summarize your approach to the markets. Think of it as your trading business plan for success. List your instruments to trade, which strategies you'll follow and how you'll expand on them.

The topics covered here only scratch the surface with regards to trading options. There are a lot more strategies to consider. Your next step would be to learn the Greeks and applying them in strategies. I'm not talking about the Iliad but the letters delta, theta, omega, alpha, and beta. You can also learn about ratio backspreads and butterfly trades. All of this sounds very exotic, but they're extremely effective.

However, before proceeding you should master the material in this book. The biggest problem for most traders is adjusting to the non-directional aspect of options. Understanding a stop loss and take profit is easy but dealing with a call option and a short put while experiencing a falling market tends to put their heads in a spin.

As always practice as much as possible before you risk real money. Even when you do begin to risk money, risk as little as possible and being by trading market neutral strategies. Once you've mastered these, move onto the more directional strategies. Meanwhile, if you do hold any long stock, employ the covered call strategy to generate some income.

Once a base is built, then you're in a good position to move forward. If the move into directional options strategies doesn't work you can always fall back on straddles and strangles along with covered calls for money making purposes. The key is to make sure your base is solid. don't move forward without it.

I hope you've enjoyed reading this book as much as I have had writing it. Options can be a dense topic to fully unpack and I've sincerely done my best to make it as foolproof as possible. Go ahead and leave me a review letting me know what you think of this book!

Lastly, I wish you the best of luck with all your trading endeavors. Keep persisting and you will meet with success.

References

Chen, J. (2019). Greeks Definition. Retrieved from https://www.investopedia.com/terms/g/greeks.asp

Dhir, R. (2019). What It Means to Exercise a Contractual Right. Retrieved from https://www.investopedia.com/terms/e/exercise.asp

Rolling Short Options | Rolling an Option Position - The Options Playbook. (2019). Retrieved from https://www.optionsplaybook.com/managing-positions/

Kenton, W. (2019). How the Black Scholes Price Model Works. Retrieved from https://www.investopedia.com/terms/b/blackscholes.asp

Vix-Index. (2019). Retrieved from http://www.cboe.com/vix

68271999R00081

Made in the USA
Columbia, SC
05 August 2019